The Quarter Circle 81

Frank Ferguson

The Quarter Circle 81

Tall Tales and Memories
Prescott & Camp Wood, Arizona
1883 - 1912

Revised Edition
Researched and Edited by
C. Robert Ferguson

Illustrated by
Susanna Kwan

BAC
P
Inc.

"The Quarter Circle 81, Tall Tales and Memories, Prescott & Camp Wood, Arizona, 1883-1912"
by Frank Ferguson
Revised Edition
Researched and Edited by C. Robert Ferguson
Illustrated by Susanna Kwan

Cover and book design by Larry W. Bledsoe

Published by: BAC Publishers, Inc.
                 1749 W. 13th St.
                 Upland, CA 91786
Manufactured in the United States of America

Originally published as "Tall Tales and Memories" by the Hassayampa Press --
Copyright © 1987 by the Estate of Frank Harris Ferguson

Library of Congress Cataloging-in-Publication Data
Ferguson, Frank, 1904-1988.
The Quarter Circle 81 : Tall Tales and Memories, Prescott &Camp Wood, Arizona, 1883-1912 / Frank Ferguson ; researched and edited by C. Robert Ferguson ; illustrated by Susanna Kwan.-- Rev. ed.
p. cm.
Rev. ed. of: Tall tales and memories. Hassayampa Press, c1987.
Summary: "These tales came down through the family that lived them and give the reader a view of Prescott and Camp Wood, Arizona, from 1883-1912"--Provided by publisher.
ISBN 0-9655730-4-4 (alk. paper)
1. Prescott Region (Ariz.)--Social life and customs--Anecdotes. 2. Ranch life--Arizona--Prescott Region--Anecdotes. 3. Outdoor life--Arizona--Prescott Region--Anecdotes. 4. Prescott Region (Ariz.)--Biography--Anecdotes. 5. Ferguson, Frank, 1904-1988--Family--Anecdotes. I. Ferguson, C. Robert. II. Ferguson, Frank, 1904-1988. Tall tales and memories. III. Title.

F819.P9F47 2004
979.1'57--dc22
2004024711

ISBN 0-9655730-4-4

First printing 2005

To my wife, Ruth, and son, Bob,
whose encouragement and help
were essential.

Table of Contents

Author's Introduction

Any similarity between the characters in this book and real persons is not coincidental, it's intentional. All of the characters were either known to the author or were characters in stories told by raconteurs whose abilities for stretching the truth were without limit. The author hopes that he has slighted no one and, if he has, he trusts that no offense will be taken, either by those living or dead, since the preservation of an endangered literary species, the tall tale, which otherwise may become extinct, is essential to American letters.

FOREWORD

My Dad was born November 7, 1904 in Prescott, Arizona. As he states in his Introduction, this book contains "tall tales." What you must remember is that he initially learned or experienced most of the events described in this book between 1904 and 1912 while he lived at the Quarter Circle 81 Ranch in Arizona, before he was eight years old, and that this book was written during 1986-87. To put this in perspective, Dad could read and write before he started school in 1910. His memory was remarkable. His experience during his lifetime was vast. He was at home on a horse, trout fishing on the Snake River in Idaho, sipping wine at a sidewalk café in Paris, or listening to a symphony on a summer night in the Hollywood Bowl.

Dad's experience was not gained easily. Dad's mother was killed in an automobile accident in 1915 after his family moved to Long Beach, California. Until my grandfather's death in 1932, my Dad lived with his father. This is one of the reasons the stories stayed fresh in my Dad's memory. My grandfather was just over 60 when they left Prescott, and he was beginning to go blind with glaucoma and cataracts. He and my father might have been living in

Long Beach, but my grandfather's heart and soul were in Arizona.

Sometime after my grandmother's accident the value of the collateral from the sale of the Quarter Circle 81 evaporated and both Dad and his father had to work. Dad first worked delivering such things as eggs and newspapers. He worked as a fruit picker in high school, a shipyard riveter during college, and an oil well pipe-puller before graduating from law school at the University of Southern California. He also managed to find time to earn high school and college letters in water polo and football, keep his golf score in the 70s and be a founding member and president of the U.S.C. chapter of Chi Phi Fraternity.

My grandfather, as you read in the stories under the title "Some People Who Built Railroads," went to work supervising the laying of track between Long Beach and San Diego for the Southern Pacific Railroad.

My Mom and Dad were married in Long Beach, California in 1933, the day after the Long Beach earthquake. Dad was working in a Los Angeles law firm at the time. He stayed there for six years and then spent three years as a trial attorney with the Los Angeles City Attorney's office. For the next thirty-one years he worked in the movie and entertainment industry. He retired in 1970 as West Coast Resident Counsel and an officer at Twentieth Century Fox Film Corporation. He was a founding member and past president of the Los Angeles Copyright Society, president of the Far West Ski Association, and a charter member of Legion Lex, the U.S.C. Law School alumni support group.

As a family, we spent a lot of time skiing, fishing, and mountaineering in the Sierra Nevada mountains. After Prescott, Dad never lived anywhere but the city. But he never really left the wilderness. He often went mountaineering in the High Sierras west of Bishop, California, just south of Mammoth Mountain, when the road was only one lane and barely paved. We began skiing Mammoth Mountain, which now has over twenty chair lifts, in the 1940s when it had only one rope tow. At that time, you didn't drive in, you rode a World War II snow vehicle called a "weasel."

My father died (fell asleep) on January 1, 1988, in front of the TV during the U.S.C. Rose Bowl game. Ironically, he had just finished his final version of this book two weeks earlier.

What follows are a series of vignettes. They are, as the title of this book states, tall tales and memories. By themselves they are fascinating. When you consider that they were written by my father in 1987 and happened seventy-five years ago, they are remarkable. The stories are in no particular order. Only the first and last stories are chronological. Thus, you might read about Camp Wood and the Quarter Circle 81 first to get a feeling for the time and place. Then all that is necessary is that you cast your mind back to the Old West, open the book to any story, and then enjoy a reflection of something that happened or was told around a campfire.

If you are a student of the time or the place, please don't quibble if my father has one or several of the facts in a story wrong. If you had pointed it out, he might have agreed with you. What he wouldn't have told you is whether it was written that way because he forgot or because he thought it made a better story.

C. *Robert Ferguson*
(January 1988)

Frank Harris Ferguson
1967

FOREWORD TO
REVISED EDITION

After re-reading Dad's book sixteen years later, I realized that because the stories were his, they omitted background that would help a reader who enjoyed reading about The West, but did not know the details of my family, Prescott, Arizona, or the surrounding area. To put things in perspective, I have added a Foreword to several of the stories. These are based on family history or sources that are noted at the end of the book. I added an Epilogue after my Dad's "Reflections on a Cattleman" (his father) because the story, as my Dad had told it several times, was incomplete. An Epilogue was added to "Mouse -- It Depends on How You Look at It" because it depends on how you look at it.

C. Robert Ferguson
(July 2004)

ACKNOWLEDGEMENTS

My Dad wrote this book to preserve a way a life and memories that were unknown to either my mother or me. Little did he know that by preparing this Revised Edition, he would provide me with a glimpse of my grandfather, who died five years before I was born, and my grandmother "Lizzie" who was killed in an automobile accident when my Dad was only eleven years old. This was an unintended consequence for which I am grateful.

Many thanks go to Michael Wurtz, Archivist at the Sharlot Hall Museum, and the Sharlot Hall Museum, Prescott, Arizona, for their help checking census data, for locating, providing, and confirming other general information about Prescott between 1883 and 1912, and for their photographs that are reproduced throughout the book.

Mona Lange McCroskey's help was invaluable. She provided extensive personal knowledge of Prescott, and insight into the era, and life at Camp Wood at the Yolo Ranch.

Lorrie Crawford can't be thanked enough for providing me with the right books to look through for my grandparents' Marriage Certificate and the original Quarter Circle 81 Registry in the Yavapai County Recorder's Office.

Thanks also go to Larry and Jane Bledsoe of BAC Publishers, Inc. It was with their help that this Edition became possible.

Ironically, it was my mother Ruth Ferguson who got this Edition started by asking, "Can we ever really finish Frank's book?"

Finally, my wife Peggy's patience and encouragement made this endeavor, its research and investigation, an adventure.

[crf]

The Quarter Circle 81

Tall Tales and Memories
Prescott & Camp Wood, Arizona
1883 - 1912

The Quarter Circle 81 Ranch

CAMP WOOD AND THE QUARTER CIRCLE 81

Camp Wood was a spot on the map about 50 miles west and north of Prescott. It was about 5,200 feet high and was an area in which there was much game. A number of quail coveys lived close to the house, deer were plentiful, and the road in front of the house afforded a trail for bears. They traveled to and fro and most of the time they created little problem, but once in a while one developed an appetite for calves and he presented a real problem so that steps had to be taken. More about the bears later.

Camp Wood was home to my family, two vaqueros (pronounced 'baquero'), miscellaneous dogs, many horses, and, initially, longhorn cattle. It was also home to two pet raccoons, and at another time, a deodorized spotted skunk. It was where I learned to ride, and where I experienced many, many things that small boys remember. Although now, after over seventy years, I'm not sure what is fact and what is fiction. After all, the long winter nights provided an atmosphere in which the tellers of tall tales were at their best. Some of the things that I remember are probably the stories that were told, not things that actually happened.

THE RANCH HOUSE, A WORK OF ART

The house at Camp Wood was made of hewn logs, two stories tall, a monument to the craftsmen who knew how to use a broadaxe and an adz. It was 'L' shaped. The downstairs consisted of one bedroom, the living room, a dining room, and the kitchen. The kitchen and the dining room were separated only by the colors of the linoleum, but the kitchen was off limits to everybody except my mother, father, Cheng, the Chinese cook, Snyder Jackson, the beagle, and to Sport, an Australian sheep dog, a sort of blue dog with black spots. With a little bleach he could masquerade as a Dalmatian. He did almost everything but talk.

The logs of which the house was built were felled on the hill which was to the south of the valley in which the ranch was located. They were probably yellow pine with some Rocky Mountain Douglas fir, and a cedar tree or two to furnish the wood for the doors, the window sills, and door sills. These trees were cut in the wintertime, and the slash was later removed and burned. They were then probably snaked into the general location where it was intended to build the house. Here they were racked up off the ground and permitted to dry until the following summer. They were then squared; that is, the sides, the tops, and the bottoms were trimmed or cut in such a manner as to leave the logs square. This was what was known as hewn logs. They could be used then in sections similar to large bricks, rather than logs as they are usually used in connection with a log cabin. I believe the only tools that the workmen had or that they actually used in this hewing operation was a cross-cut saw, a broadaxe, an adz, and of course a chalk line and a level. Since it was necessary that the logs be relatively square, a carpenter's square was needed.

Any minor defects in this regard could be corrected by the use of line mortar which was used for chinking. The logs, as they were hoisted into place, were fastened with pins which were made of oak. The holes in which they were inserted were probably drilled with a two-inch auger, each log being fastened to the one below it until the proper height was reached. Then the roof was framed, and it was finished with shakes which were made from cedar that was probably felled in the same general location as the logs which formed the structure of the house.

The cabinet work was done separately by a craftsman who was handy with tools. The cupboards were well designed and well placed.

The doors fitted beautifully, and the inside of the house was lined with a sort of sheeting which was similar to tongue and groove flooring, only much thinner. This was painted and made a beautiful interior. There were many windows, and the interior was well lighted and cheerful. As I said before, the house was the work of skilled and dedicated craftsmen who obviously enjoyed what they were doing, and did it well.

The second story included a hall and four bedrooms.

Along the long part of the 'L', facing north, was a roofed-over porch. At the end of the porch was the well. I understand the well was dug first and then the house was built so that the well would be adjacent and handy to the kitchen. The floor of the porch was slabs, probably Jeffrey pine, which had some knots in the wood, some of which were punched out. These holes afforded an endless challenge to the raccoons. They could never pass one without feeling underneath to see what was down the knothole. Nothing was ever found.

As one stood on the porch of the Quarter Circle 81 ranch house and looked out over the shallow valley, a small stream flowed down in front of the house about 50 yards away, and across the stream, approximately equidistant, was a large barn, and further to the east a huge corral built of peeled logs. To the west of the barn and further north was the blacksmith shop which was adjoined by a bunkhouse, and a storage house where meat and other supplies were kept.

The ranch house was heated by two enormous stoves; one was in the kitchen and had a water tank on one side with coils that went through the fire box. This was where Cheng was king, and this is where he operated. The other stove, which also had a water tank and coils, was a big pot-bellied number in the living room, which was usually referred to as the parlor. The pipes of both of these stoves were so arranged that the upstairs rooms were heated when there were fires in the stoves. It was this arrangement which caused the fire which burned down this beautiful ranch house in about 1910. That was really an experience and deserves detailed treatment.

JERKY

Jerky played an important part in everyone's diet, both at the ranch house, on roundup trips and in cow camps all over The West. When a beef was killed, the meat was hung out and cooled at night. Then, in the daytime, it was brought into the house where it was wrapped in blankets, or quilts (comforts), and tarpaulins and kept cool during the course of the day, to be hung out again at night. This practice permitted the keeping of meat without refrigeration for a substantial period of time. After a while, when this process was no longer effective, what remained was cut into long strips, salted, peppered, and hung out in the wind and sun to dry. It was not smoked. Smoke was only used if it was necessary to keep the blowflies away from the jerky.

To prepare jerky for a meal, the dried jerky was beaten on an anvil, usually with a horseshoeing or ball peen hammer. This separated the fascia, or gristly tissue. The lean portion of the jerky was then mixed in a cream sauce, very much like a cream gravy, and served over fresh biscuits. It was good any time of the day, and it was used as a dish for breakfast, dinner, which was served always in the middle of the day, or supper, which came at night.

At roundup time, particularly, I can remember Cheng beating jerky on the anvil in the blacksmith's shop. He really went to work at it. He used a ball peen hammer and could turn out a lot of beaten jerky in a relatively short period of time. In this operation he always had an audience - all the dogs sat around in a half circle waiting for pieces of fascia to be tossed or pushed off the anvil. This, apparently, was gourmet food for canines, and whenever they heard a noise in the blacksmith's shop that sounded like someone beating on the anvil they all congregated. I remember one particular time when my father was straightening a bunch of nails (these, as I recall, were rectangular rather than round and when used, the flat side was driven parallel to the grain so the wood wouldn't split.) He had quite an audience of dogs. The only difference was that there was no edible food and it was not long until they were discouraged and left. He laughed about this a number of times -- about how straightening nails always brought the pooches, and how their patience was always short.

CATTLE AND DOGS (SNYDER JACKSON)

During the short period that I lived at Camp Wood the cattle were in a state of transition, from long legged progeny of their Texas forebears to white faced Herefords. For beef on the Ranch, normally a motley faced yearling Hereford heifer was butchered. When a beef was butchered all of the parts normally unobtainable in butcher shops were first used. This involved the sweetbreads (which I believe is the pancreas,) the liver, the tongue, and another piece of viscera known as treepers.[1] I'm not sure what they were, but I think they were the milk intestines which had become no longer useful after the calf was weaned. This was considered a real delicacy and I have never heard of it anywhere except on ranches which butcher their own beeves. The brains were scrambled with eggs. The use of these various parts afforded an opportunity to hang the meat at least for a few days and let it age slightly. After all, it was not fattened the way the meat is that

---

[1] *Tripas de leche*

we obtain today. Beeves which we butchered were sometimes grass fattened on hilaria and grama grass, but primarily they fed on the oak bush which formed a browse for the deer and was fine cattle food on which the yearlings and two-year-olds got fat and sassy. It was the fat and sassy heifers that were normally butchered. Steers were too valuable.

The dogs at Camp Wood served a real purpose. They were a very important adjunct to the cattle operation in the early days when good hands were hard to come by. Each dog performed some function that was really worthwhile; that is, with the exception of Snyder Jackson, who was actually my mother's pet. He was more ornamental than useful and actually was the only dog permitted to sleep in the house. At night, he occupied an old sofa in the hall where the stairway went up to the second floor, and he had the luxury of being covered up by a Navajo blanket. If he kicked it off, he came in and woke up someone and went and got back on his bed so that he could be re-covered. He was really a pet dog.

Sport, the spotted blue dog, was a herding dog and his function when cattle were being moved from one place to another was to round up the little calves that hid in the thick brush. The herders would stop the parada, hold them, and send Sport back to search for tired calves. He would work the brush just like a bird dog and come out with all the little calves that had gone down.

Two other dogs were Colonel and Major. Colonel was a black dog, who my father said wasn't worth a damn. But he actually earned his keep by keeping the skunks under control and making sure they never raided the hen house, with a net result he always had a slightly high odor, sometimes higher than others, and was never welcome on the porch or in the house. Major, his sibling, was a brindle dog, and when a little calf would break out, he would be sent to get him. What would happen is he would chase the calf, grab him by the jaw, and sit down. A herder could then leisurely go out and round up the calf and put him back in the herd. This performance was really amusing when the calf was as large or larger than the dog. But Major was pretty persistent and pretty effective, and it was seldom that he let one get away.

Snyder Jackson came into his own when corn was being harvested. The cornfield was west of the house, not too far from the meadow where the little stream began. The corn was cut and shocked and permitted to cure so that the stocks and leaves would be fodder. When the shocks were dried, they were hauled in and stored in the barn. During the drying period, field mice set up nests under each of the shocks and Snyder Jackson had a field day catching the mice as the shocks were picked up and thrown into the wagon. I used to insist that he give up part of his prizes so that the cats could be fed with the field mice. This always amused my father.

Snyder Jackson and Sport each indulged in a practice which resulted in the woodpile inside the house being replenished. Each would go get a stick of wood, rattle it against the back door until Cheng let him in. Snyder Jackson and Sport would each put his stick of wood down and, if he were instructed, would get his own biscuit out of the biscuit box. Neither dog would give my father the stick of wood until he produced a biscuit. This was always a source of much amusement to Cheng. How this practice originated, I don't know. But I must assume that at some time or another my father played a trick on one or the other or both of the dogs, and from then on it was a pay or play operation.

THE POST OFFICE

Camp Wood, in the early days, was a post office. My father was the postmaster from about 1893 to 1907. It didn't pay much and I often heard him say that as postmaster his pay consisted of the stamps that he canceled. This operation was probably profitable when the Hillside Mine was in operation, since all the mining correspondence cleared through the Camp Wood Post Office. After the mine closed, its only patrons were the people at Camp Wood, and the ranchers at the Pitchfork, the Yolo, and the sheep ranch, which were all within a ten-mile radius.

I suspect that the original Camp Wood location was selected because it was about a full day's travel from Prescott by buckboard and about half way between Prescott and the location of the Hillside Mine. During the early days when my parents were homesteading the place, my mother ran a station stop for the stage which went on to the Hillside Mine, and my father spent most of his time working for the Atlantic and Pacific Railroad, which subsequently became the Santa Fe.

HiBEE: THE BLACK AND WHITE FURRY FRIEND

I'm not sure how HiBee arrived at Camp Wood, or exactly where he came from. I remember him first when one early spring morning Manuel came into the house with his overcoat on and asked my mother in Spanish if she would like a pet. She replied, "What is it?" whereupon he produced this small, black, spotted, furry creature. He was about the size of a half-grown cat. He was black with a white spot on his forehead and a white spot under each ear. There were broken spots along his sides and down his back. He was a small, spotted skunk, about half grown, gentle and completely odorless. Manuel put him down and he seemed to be perfectly at home. Snyder Jackson came into the room and barked and HiBee immediately assumed the position which resulted in his name, High Behind - a handstand on his front feet with his tail in the air and a threatening look, "Don't come closer." Someone chased the dog out of the room and Manuel picked up HiBee and put him back in his pocket. Shortly afterwards, he took him out again and the skunk seemed perfectly at home. He was not afraid of people and he was gentle, did not object to being picked up, and seemed to enjoy being petted and fussed over. From then on, he was actually part of the family. How my father trained the dogs to leave him alone I'm not sure, but none of them ever bothered him.

HiBee was pretty nocturnal. He was active at night, loved to sleep in the daytime, and was really no problem. He was completely housebroken and was a much better pet than some of the other animals that I have known from time to time. When he was full grown, he weighed about a pound and a half. His body was about nine inches long and he was just the right size to fit into a small boy's blouse, which got me in trouble later on in kindergarten.

HiBee's diet was comparable to the cats', except he augmented it with insects. He was a good mouse catcher and occasionally Cheng would reward him with what I'm sure to him was an ice cream cone. It was a mixture of a dish of cream and a raw egg beaten together. This was eaten not only by lapping it up with his tongue, but by dipping in one paw and then licking the paw. I've seen monkeys do this, and I've seen a few cats do it, but with HiBee it was a constant practice. He also searched the rocks and crannies along the creek bed. Here he captured small frogs and aquatic insects. These also augmented the normal diet of things similar to those fed to the cats. HiBee had another favorite hunting place - the woodpile. He dug around in the chips and small sticks and unearthed grub worms -- big white fellows with yellow heads -- which he devoured with great gusto. These were apparently apple pie and ice cream for skunks.

One day Ramon Contreras put him down close to a red ant hill. He didn't like the ants at all and he didn't like Ramon for weeks after that. He wouldn't let Ramon pick him up or come close. Without the normal skunk's defensive capabilities he would have made a good meal for a coyote had he been out loose, running around, rooting here and there for grubs and insects in normal skunk fashion.

One day when HiBee was about three-quarters grown, he performed a trick which became a part of his behavior pattern and stayed with him, I think, for the rest of his life. I reached down to pick him up and he jumped so that I caught him in my arms. From then on, all you had to do was walk by or walk up to him, make a basket of your arms and he'd jump up and you could catch him without any problem.

Small boy outfits at the time consisted of bib overalls and large pockets, very much like the ones Dennis the Menace in the funny paper wears today. I put him in the pocket of my overalls one day and was surprised to find that he seemed to be perfectly at home there and perfectly content. I was carrying him one day when Ramon looked at me and started in laughing and remarked that my friend had on a white cap. I looked down and, sure enough, the tip of his tail was up over the top of his head so the little, bright-eyed rascal appeared to have a white cap on, or at least a visor, which partially covered his bright, beady eyes. It didn't seem to make any difference how you put him in your pocket, he always managed to squirm around so that both ends of the skunk were out and he was perfectly content to stay there for the balance of the day. I think that it was this feeling of security, which was lacking the time I took him to school in the roll of my blouse. It wasn't quite like the deep pants pocket, and he wasn't too happy. Probably, had I had on the bib overalls which he had grown accustomed to when I took him to school, he would have stayed put, and I would have had no problems and he could have continued his education in my kindergarten class.

When I moved off the ranch and went to Prescott with my mother, I persuaded everyone that HiBee should go along, too. This was discouraged at first, but apparently somebody gave in and let me take him, since there was a small cage that was portable and I could keep him in the house where we lived on Union Street.

I took him to school with me one day in the blouse that I wore, which was typical of the garments of small school boys in those days. As I remember, I was, I believe, five. HiBee, some way or another, got out, ran over in the corner, and immediately threatened everyone in the room. I picked him up and was taken to the principal's office. HiBee and I went home and my instructions were to leave him there and, believe me, I did. That was the end of his education, but he really didn't need one anyway.

Now that I think about it, the bib overalls might not have worked. Skunks, and particularly spotted skunks, have a bad reputation as hydrophobia carriers. This is probably true due to the fact that they are almost fearless and rely entirely upon their normal defense to keep enemies at bay. A rabid animal probably disregards this danger and attacks them, with resulting infection.

HiBee was still alive when the Quarter Circle 81 was sold and Manuel Altaininano took him with him to the Kinsavy Ranch in Burro Creek, where I understand, he became a companion for Leonard Neal and was a source of great amusement to the Neal family until he died at the age of about seven or eight. I gather that HiBee lived a long, eventful, and happy life. He was a wonderful little fellow.

Frontier Days and "The World Record"

Everyone from Quarter Circle 81 tried to be in Prescott, Arizona for the 4th of July. This was for Frontier Days, which is actually the oldest organized rodeo in the United States. It was well-established when the Cheyenne, Wyoming, rodeo started and when the Calgary Stampede was inaugurated. Frontier Days in Prescott involved all the usual bronc riding and steer bull-dogging, but the most fun for me were the relay races. These were team affairs, four men to a team.

As I recall, the race consisted of two laps around a half-mile track. The horses and saddles had to be changed at the end of each quarter mile. The trick was to take the saddle off of one horse and throw it onto another, mount and ride the quarter mile with a loose cinch and still stay aboard. This took a lot of horsemanship, and there were very few people who could accomplish it. Most of the time, rigs were arranged so that dallying the latigo around the horn would hold a saddle sufficiently to enable the rider to negotiate the quarter mile. I think these relay races were in many ways comparable to the chuck wagon races which so typified the Calgary Stampede.

Another event which was unique to the Frontier Days in Prescott was the steer roping. Steer roping was so unique, and so much a part of Prescott that it was going on the whole time we lived in Prescott, even though the legislature had made it illegal several years before I was born. Steer roping involved the use of two- and three-year-old steers, which were normally roped by two men, thrown, and hog-tied. It wasn't a calf roping the way it's usually done now, but actually involved the handling of full grown cattle. It took not only a great deal of skill, but horses that were excellently trained and men who knew their horses and knew how to handle the animals that they were pitted against.

Manuel Altaininano and Ramon held the record for a short period of time. I believe at that time it was considered to be the World's Championship. The fact of the matter is that it probably was, since the event was held in no other place in the world. So, it probably was the World's Championship if you want to be a little parochial about it.

*Sharlot Hall Museum photo,
Prescott, Arizona*

Steer Roping ca 1904

REFLECTIONS ON A CATTLEMAN

FOREWORD

My grandfather, Robert Hannibal Ferguson, was born in Monroe County, Tennessee in 1851. His family left Tennessee in 1865 and moved to Missouri where they continued the farming and cattle business. My grandfather left Missouri in 1875, lived in Colorado for a while, then moved to Prescott in the early 1880s. He and my Grandmother, Elizabeth "Lizzie" Harris were married in June 1886. As you can see from the dates, my grandfather was in his 20s and 30s during the 1870s and 80s when the Old West was at its height. His ranch, the Quarter Circle 81, was a relatively large ranch and my grandfather knew many of the major players of the era, including the Earp family and Wild Bill Hickock. [crf]

REFLECTIONS

One of the things that I remember with considerable amusement is the little ritual that took place when we went to Prescott. My mother and father would be shopping. When we would finish and start back to the

*The wedding photographs of Robert H. Ferguson and
Elizabeth "Lizzie" Harris [crf]*

Marriage certificate of Robert H. Ferguson and Elizabeth Harris from the records of Yavapai County, Arizona. The reason for the mis-pelling of Harris is unknown. *[crf]*

hotel, which was on Gurley Street east of Cortez, we'd get to about the corner of Cortez and Gurley and my father would say, "Liz, I'm going to go down and help the boys keep the horses out of the car barn." The little trolley that

Trolley on Gurley Street looking west toward Thumb Butte.

ran up and down Gurley Street was actually housed in a car barn on Cortez down close to the depot. The other side of the plaza, that is, a block west, was Montezuma, which from Gurley Street, south for one whole block, was Whiskey Row--one whole block of saloons. I think this was where my father usually ended up to have a drink with his old friends and to pass the time with some of the boys that he hadn't seen for a long time. Usually he'd be gone for an hour or an hour and a half and arrive home with a twinkle in his eye. That was about all it amounted to. It took me years to figure out exactly what went on. I think I was probably fourteen or fifteen before it finally dawned on me that the "horses in the car barn" were not quite in the same direction as the location of the car barn. This, I think, was what tipped me off to the actual escapade. I've laughed about it many times, and I think it's probably a pretty good comment. Keeping the horses out of the car barn should be a pleasant and amusing pastime.

My father used to bet on the Frontier Days relay races.

The bets were never much, usually just a few dollars with friends, but he seemed to win a great deal of the time and I often wondered how he did it. I asked him one time later and he chuckled and said, "You have to take into consideration all the factors -- not only the ability of the riders and the quality of the horses, but you've got to look at their conformation. The saddles have to stay on, and a flat backed horse is at a decided disadvantage or, at least the rider is at a decided disadvantage."

This was one of the things that I always looked for. If one of the teams had one or more horses that were a little bit on the flat-backed side, I figured they were unable to win, and most of the time they didn't. It worked out pretty well. Besides, it was a lot of fun, and no one else seemed to ever figure out that wrinkle.

Most little boys seem to deify their fathers, particularly if they were loved, encouraged from time to time, disciplined slightly, and probably a little bit spoiled. Thomas Wolfe paints a beautiful picture of his father in *Look Homeward Angel*, despite his idiosyncrasies of building roaring fires and shouting ringing admonitions from the top of the stairs, which resounded through the living room and over the fireplace. Over the years I have endeavored to sort of put a picture together in my own mind of the man whom I remember as riding tall in the saddle, wearing a big hat rolled slightly at the brim, and creased so that the crease was higher in the back than in the front, spurs with big pointed rowels, batwinged chaps, and tapaderos that could be slapped together under the horse's belly. The spurs came off when he dismounted, and were hung by the chains that went under the instep, over the saddle horn. The vaquero, unlike the cowboy, took off his spurs when he was on the ground. The rowels were too large and sometimes bounced along as he walked if he left them on.

My father was gentle with horses and he was an expert at bridling colts, that is, taking them through the transition period from the hackamore, to the snaffle bit, to the high-port bit that they eventually would wear the balance of their working lives. This required patience, but most of all, gentle hands and an understanding of the horse's ability. He also was able to get dogs to mind. How he did this I was never quite sure.

If you borrowed his tools, he wanted them returned in good order. If he borrowed yours, he sharpened your axe, for instance, before he gave it back. This courtesy he expected from everyone else.

He was tolerant and patient up to a point, but when this point was reached, be careful because all hell broke loose. I only saw this happen once or twice, but it left a very lasting impression.

One incident occurred in the corral when a cowboy abused one of our horses. It was really frightening. I was sitting up on the corral watching them branding calves. The cowboy was riding one of the Quarter Circle 81 string since his own horse had gone lame. Whoever had been riding the horse before the cowboy had thrown a little bit longer rope. The cowboy spurred the horse unnecessarily to get him into position and my father admonished him to be careful, and not to do it again. Nevertheless, the process was repeated and the horse was harshly spurred, with even more force. What happened afterwards left an indelible impression.

The corral at the Quarter Circle 81 was about 100 feet long and probably sixty feet wide, built of peeled logs. It was about six feet high. In other words, it was horse high and bull tight. The eastern end of the barn formed a portion of the corral, except that along the base the log fence had been continued up to about four feet. It was where the six-foot fence joined the barn that I usually viewed what went on in the corral. It was a vantagepoint which I could reach by climbing up the logs and holding onto the attachments that were fitted in between against the barn wall. It was a pretty safe place to be. Usually I got a little help and somebody said, "Here you go up; hold on tight, boy; don't fall." And it was from here that I witnessed the scene that followed.

The first thing after the second spurring was that the air literally turned blue. My father, in a burst of profanity (a perfection of which I have never heard since) consisting of a mixture of English and Spanish with a slight Southern accent and a Scottish burr, discussed the cowboy's pedigree or lack thereof, the contours of his soon-to-be carcass if he didn't behave, and the hardness which surrounded the emptiness that consisted of his head. It was a marvelous performance, and I have often thought that I have never heard an equal (not even by Joe Kennedy, the patriarch of the Kennedy family who considered himself to be quite an expert with the language, at least so he told me when we were talking forty years later). The cowboy, obviously taken aback by this verbal assault, turned slightly in the saddle, only to find himself knocked completely out of it and as he hit the ground my father landed on him. How he managed to get out of the saddle on the wrong side of the horse I have never quite understood. But anyway, the next thing I saw happen was a shirt torn to ribbons. I am sure that the cowboy still has a few scars across the ribs and between his shoulder blades. He was ordered off the ranch and instructed that if he ever appeared again, he'd be shot on sight. The last I saw of him he was vaulting over the corral gate at the other end of the corral. My father then mounted his horse, coiled his rope, pitched it over a calf, dragged him up to the branding fire and proceeded as if absolutely nothing had happened. No one said anything further about the incident, except I related it in some detail to my mother later in the day. She sort of rubbed me between the ears and said, "Don't talk about it any more. Your father can get a little angry at times." That was the understatement of the year!

EPILOGUE

There is a part of this story that my Dad told me on several occasions, but left out because he thought it made his father look like a violent man, which he wasn't.
When the cowboy turned in his saddle, it looked like he was

reaching for his gun. After my grandfather knocked the cowboy out of his saddle, the cowboy got up. My grandfather then yelled, "You're fired, now get out of here!"

The cowboy said, "You owe me back pay and I'm not leaving 'til I get it."

My grandfather then told the cowboy that he had taken his pay out on the horse. When my grandfather started walking toward him, the cowboy drew his gun on my grandfather, whose gun was back in the house. My grandfather kept walking. The cowboy with his gun still pointed at my grandfather started backing up. When one of the rowels of a spur caught in the dirt, he tripped, and events continued as they are told in the tale. [crf]

REFLECTIONS ON SOME REAL AND NOT VERY FAMOUS VAQUEROS AND COWBOYS

FOREWORD

When my Dad wrote this part of the book, I was surprised at his intensity. His description of a vaquero was very different from the general reference to a cowboy from Mexico that I had learned. I told him, and asked if he was sure about what he had written. He was emphatic □"Yes."

After re□reading what follows, I did some additional reading to see if there is a consistent definition of a vaquero. Other than vaque□ ros are of Mexican descent, it seems there is none. And since my Dad got to be head of the legal department at 20th Century Fox Film Studios by knowing what he was talking about, I leave it to others to show that his definitions do not apply to vaqueros in and about Prescott, Arizona between 1883 and 1912, when he and his father lived there. [crf]

COWBOYS, VAQUEROS AND BUCKAROOS

Camp Wood was also home to a number of bucka-roos. One was Indian Joe, who was a fine crafts-man and manufacturer of riatas. He also could work silver and made the conchas for the bridles. Another was Ed, who had started his life as a herdsman, as a cowboy, and had come into Arizona with a herd of longhorn cattle. He had switched, dropping his rimmy ways and taking up the center fire saddle, the long rope, the high port bit, and learning to handle the horses which were trained to neck rein and which maneuvered like a cavalryman's horse, not like a cowboy's horse that required both hands. These men were buckaroos. The word "buckaroo" is a corruption of the word "vaquero." Adams, in his Dictionary Of Western Words, suggests that buckaroo is synonymous with cowboy. This is probably not correct. The original buckaroos were Anglos who initially jumped ship in the 1840s and early '50s and eventually ended up working on the big ranches in the San Joaquin Valley. They worked in Nevada, and then in western Arizona, also in Montana and Wyoming. Will James had the right idea, severing the "cowboys" into two areas, but he had the areas wrong. It was east and west, not north and south.

Adams also defines the word "vaquero" as synonymous for cowboy, suggesting it was used in the Southwest. The vaqueros in Prescott had been cavalrymen on horseback who originally learned their craft in California. That whirling noise you hear is the old hands, the herders, who worked for Miller and Lux, Karem Hagan, the El Tajon, the Pitchfork, the Quarter Circle 81, the Cross Triangle, and the big ranches all over Nevada turning over in their graves. They had been cavalrymen. They were not cowboys. The basis for the system of riding used by the vaquero originally came from Spain and was known as La Jineta. It was greatly modified in the Western Hemisphere.

REFLECTIONS

Tot Young, worked for the Quarter Circle 81 as a horse wrangler when he was a young man. He was in the pasture one morning when I fell off of Mouse, a mouse-colored burro, when I was trying to round up some horses that he'd brought in from the range. He planned to put them in the corral and, since they were barefooted, to shoe them. Shoeing horses was one of the things he did well, and that was one of the reasons that he was valuable. The average cowpuncher could shoe a horse, but they were not all experts. Tot really was.

After my mother and I moved to Prescott, Tot went to work for the Cross Triangle in Williamson Valley. He was replaced by Logan Morris. Logan was older and was an expert in horse breaking. He was a bronc buster of considerable ability and his horses, when he finished with them, were gentle, well-reined, and well-behaved.

Logan's only idiosyncrasy was for names. Horses broken by Logan Morris went through life known as Buzzard Head, Tin Can, and Tomatoes. Tomatoes was a cutting horse that my cousin, John Neal, owned. John tells the story about Tomatoes and the little Chinese boy, whose family was killed in a tong war, whom he brought out to the Kinsavy ranch, and then wondered what to do with him. They put him on Tomatoes, figuring Tomatoes was a real gentle horse. The first thing Tomatoes did was take off at a full gallop. The Chinese boy reared back in the saddle, yelling, "Whoa, Tomatoes," and everyone swears to this day that his eyes were not almond but as round as dollars. He won't deny this, and if you don't believe it, just ask him. He runs a wonderful restaurant in Kingman.

One of the best cowboys at the Quarter Circle 81, if not the best, was a black cowboy named Ed.[1] Ed, my father, and Abe Goodman were up in the Hyde Creek drainage attempting to round up some big orejana steers. The steers up there were three to five years old or older, and had been missed by many roundups. They were as wild as wild animals, and presented a real problem to the cow punchers who were trying to round them up to ship on their way to the packing house.

The technique is to lasso them, hog-tie them, dehorn them—that is, cut off at least the tips of the horns, rub off the sharp edge with a rock, tie the steer up to a juniper tree with a short length of rope so that he can only stand up or lie down, and then leave him for two or three days until he reaches a point of exhaustion. After this time the steer can usually be led, and two men can bring him back to civilization. It's tricky work, and Ed was very good at it.

But one time Ed got his rope on a big orejana and his horse stumbled and fell. The horse got up, Ed didn't.

---

[1] *His full name back in the late 1800s and early 1900s was Nigger Ed. [crf]*

When my father and Goodman got to him, the first question was, "What's the matter?"

Ed said, "My leg's broke." Goodman started to pull out his six shooter and Ed said, "Mr. Goodman, what are you doin'?"

Goodman's reply was, "Can't get a horse or its rider with a broken leg down off this mountain. There's nothing to do but shoot him."

Whereupon Ed replied, "Wait a minute, Mr. Goodman, maybe it ain't broke."

It turned out it wasn't broken. It was only sprained. But Ed still couldn't ride without a lot of help. It was slow, but they were able to get him down just fine. The mountain on which this happened was next to Hyde Creek Mountain and became known throughout that part of Arizona as Nigger Ed Mountain. It carried that name for years and years. Recently, some geographer didn't like the name, and I believe the name has been changed to Black Man's Mountain.[2] I'm sure if anyone had ever asked Ed what he wanted to do about it, he would have said, "Just let the tail go with the hide." Just leave the name the way it is.

WHO EATS IN THE DINING ROOM

One day my father sent Indian Joe with four saddle horses over to the Yolo Ranch, which was about four miles away. When he got back, my mother asked him, "Joe, have you had dinner?"

He said, "Yes, I had dinner."

---

2. *To many old timers in Prescott, the original name has stuck. [crf]*

My mother said, "Where'd you eat?

Indian Joe said, "Out on the porch. All same dog. Little different from here, Aunt Lizzie."

And that was that. My father never asked Joe or Ed to go to the Yolo again. My father was very sensitive about such things. He measured men by their performance, not by their color or by their creed. Good men ate in the dining room, not out on the porch.

MORE ABOUT A REAL COWBOY

A lot has been said about black cowboys, and I have been asked if I have any more biographical data on Ed. I don't have a great deal. I only knew that when he worked at the Quarter Circle 81 he was about fifty years old. He had come into Arizona as a cowboy out of Texas. When he arrived there he rode a double-cinched saddle, the end of his rope was tied to his saddle horn, his spurs carried the small rowels of the Texas cowboy, he handled his horse with a low-port or snaffle-type bit, and he was dressed as cowboys dressed, with relatively flat hats. As I remember, his chaps (pronounced 'shaps') were batwing. Of course batwing chaps were worn by both vaqueros and cowboys, but they were more a cowboy affectation than vaquero. His accent was not Texan. He lacked the drawl that is so typical of Texas, and it was a softer note. I have a feeling that he grew up in the Carolinas. His family had been slaves and he had been freed, of course, as a result of the Civil War. He was probably about thirteen or fourteen when the war was over, and I have no idea how he emigrated, from wherever it was that he originated, into Texas. But he was one of the black cowboys that worked in the Texas Panhandle. And, although I never heard him talk about it, it's quite probable that he was one of the cowboys that participated in the cattle drives from the Panhandle to Dodge City and Abilene. He certainly was a trail herder as evidenced by the fact that it was generally known that he arrived in Prescott as a trail herder from Texas. The herd that he arrived with came from somewhere in the vicinity of Amarillo, was driven across the staked plains in New Mexico, and across New Mexico into Arizona. This technique was the way cattle were transported not only into Arizona, but also into Wyoming and into Colorado, and to a very small extent into Nevada.

THE WORLD
BELONGS TO
RACCOONS

We had two pet raccoons. I was never as friendly with them as I was with HiBee the skunk, but
I used to observe them from time to time, and
there were so many tales told about their mischievousness
that I am really not sure as to what I actually witnessed and
what I heard about them. One of the things that they used

to do -- and this I have seen many times -- was to hunt for frogs along the little stream that ran down in front of the house. One raccoon would get into the water, and the other would stay up on the bank. The one in the water would move very slowly and carefully along and when he could manage it, he would throw a frog out on the bank. The raccoon on the bank would grab it before it could get back in. They would then rip the frog open and clean it -- just like a person would clean a fish before they ate him. Raccoons are reputed to wash everything before they eat it. This they do, but I believe it is due to a shortness of saliva or a lack of proper functioning of their saliva glands that brings this about. I have actually seen them in zoos take a grape over and wash it before eating it. On one occasion, I watched one eat a grape and then go wash his hands, so I'm not sure but that it is somewhat of a reflex action.

The porch in front of the house had been built out of slab lumber, which meant that there were some knots in it. These knots had, from time to time, been pushed out, leaving knotholes. And it didn't make any difference how many times a raccoon went by a knothole, it always had to reach in and feel around as if it was searching for something. On one occasion I happened to be under the porch when one little black paw came down through a knothole and I grabbed it. The screaming, yelling, crying, and wailing that went on was unimaginable. Needless to say, I quickly let go and the raccoon beat a hasty retreat. But it didn't stop him from reaching down the same knothole the next time he went by three days later.

Another pet trick was to grab a hat if somebody left one where it was readily accessible and didn't hang it up in the front hall. If the raccoon could get his hands on it, he'd take it outside and make a mess in it. This seemed to be a standard practice, and a number of cowboy hats of passers-by who didn't realize the risk or danger were ruined. Everybody around the ranch was careful; hats were hung up on hooks or little hat racks where they belonged.

John Neal inadvertently discovered a ploy of the raccoons that amused everyone for a number of months. He playfully gave one of them one of my father's old pipes. The raccoon smelled it and ran out to the stream and proceeded to wash it. He washed for about an hour and a half, smelling about every ten minutes and then washing some more. As a matter of fact, he spent the whole afternoon washing, and John Neal said from then on that if he ever wanted to keep one or both of them busy, just supply them with an old pipe, and you have absolutely nothing to worry about for quite a long time. I think this was probably correct. They never did learn that they couldn't wash the tobacco smell out of an old pipe. Particularly some old corncob.

The raccoons had been fairly young when they were first brought to the ranch. As they grew older they spent less and less time in the general vicinity of the ranch house. After my mother and I had gone to Prescott so that I could go to school, both of them disappeared. One was never seen again, but the other little raccoon eventually showed up with her family and hung around for a couple of days. She was fairly friendly, although she was nothing like she had been when she was a permanent resident. This lasted, according to my father, for about a week. Then she too went back to whatever she was doing before she came back to pay a visit.

Comments About Horses

Horses played a very important part in the lives of the people at the Quarter Circle 81. Two that I remember very distinctly were Blackman and Hobson. They were two of my father's favorites. Blackman was, as his name suggested, a jet black horse with a white star on his forehead. He was about fifteen-and-a-half hands high and was as quick as a big cat. Hobson was named for Richmond Pierson Hobson who, I was told, was the commander of the Merrimac, which was sunk by the Monitor during the Civil War. He was a sorrel horse with four white stockings. He was about the same size as Blackman, not as gentle, but probably a little quicker. He was my father's favorite cutting horse. Neither one of these was ever ridden by anyone else other than possibly by Manuel and Ramon. There were a number of other horses broken by various horse wranglers from time to time, and they constituted the string that the cowpunchers used.

My string of horses over the years consisted of Mouse, the burro; a big horse (about fifteen hands) named

Morgan; and Dobbin. Morgan had been a top cow horse in his day and subsequently became my mother's favorite horse. She rode him for many years with a side saddle. I inherited him. When they put my postage stamp saddle on him they had to extend the latigo on both sides so that the cinch would go around him. My problem was to get on him. I used to have to get him up alongside the fence, climb up the fence and then mount. I think if I'd ever fallen off he would have probably figured out a way to put me back on. He was as gentle as a dog, very careful, and beautifully gaited. The only trouble was he was just too big a horse for such a small boy.

The horse that I eventually came to love was a little Indian pony that had been broken by the Yavapais and ridden by the children of the Yavapai families. I think my father traded one of his best horses for him. The Indians, for some unknown reason, had named him Dobbin, which didn't any more fit him than the name would fit a whippet. But he could run like the wind and used to love to race with anybody who'd race with me when we could get a good open stretch of terrain. One of the favorite places was down the road when you were coming home from Pine Flat or back home from the Pitchfork or the Yolo. There was a good quarter mile on each side before you got home that was fairly level, and this was a great place for Dobbin and me to show everyone else our heels. In retrospect, I suspect that a lot of people let me win. But nevertheless, Dobbin was like Sea Biscuit. He wasn't very big, but he was awfully fast.

THE THREE BEARS,
AND A FEW MORE

The "three bears" is really three separate bear stories.

The first bear story involves a bearskin which was stretched out on the parlor or living room floor. It was a big rug, and it covered a lot of area. The hair on the ruff of the neck, or the part of the hump which is so typical of the grizzly, stood up like hackles. This bear must have really been mad and, from what I hear, I suspect he was. He had killed a calf in the corral and dragged it out over the top of the six foot high log corral fence. My father set a trap for him and eventually caught him. But, some way or another, this bear got the trap up through a fork in a juniper tree and was making a great deal of noise early in the morning, about 3:00 or 4:00 a.m. My father went out to see what was in the trap and soon discovered the bear. He shot him with a Sharp's rifle. I think it was a 45/70, which means that it threw a bullet almost as big in diameter as a dime. The bullet cut the main artery in the bear's heart and tore out part of the heart. The bear took a good ten minutes to die. My father said that if the bear had

43

been able to attack him, he could have killed him three times over. This was the bear that made the living room rug, and it was quite a rug.

The second story should be called "Big Foot." One morning, Manuel came into the kitchen with his eyes as big as saucers, telling about the bear tracks he'd seen in the road. They were from the biggest grizzly bear that ever lived, according to him, and as soon as breakfast was over everybody adjourned to the road to look at the bear tracks. The verdict was unanimous, it was the biggest bear track anyone had ever seen. I was no judge, but it looked like a big bear track to me and since everyone else agreed, it was. I was certain that this bear must be as big as the hairy mammoth. Shortly afterwards, Pete White, a professional hunter, came along and was regaled with the stories of the size of the bear. "I'll look for him," he said when he took off, and the next day he set out with his pack animal to see if he could locate the biggest bear in all of Christendom.

About a week later he came back, leading a pack mule, obviously with something packed between the kyacks. What it was it was difficult to tell since it was covered with a tarpaulin.

Anyway, Pete rode up to the hitch rack, got off, tied his horse, pulled the mule up and tied him to the hitch rack, and started to take off the pack. As he undid the diamond hitch, the mule shied and a bear paw the size of a meat platter slid down the mule's shoulder. He proceeded right then and there to buck everything off all over the place. The actual bearskin was about the size of a good sized dog. The bear was all feet. Everyone looked on in amazement, and finally someone said, "What happened, Pete? How would you account for the size of the bear's feet as compared to the size of the bear?"

"I don't know," he said. "My only solution is that he must have been inbred."

Needless to say, White received a bounty for the bear, but the bear did not end up on anyone's floor as a rug, nor were the claws sold as souvenirs. What happened to them, I can only speculate, but I suspect that some Indian medicine man had them for years as his prized possession.

The third bear taught me when to stand up and when to back off. One afternoon, about two o'clock, my father rode in, unsaddled his horse and came over to the house. My mother greeted him and told him she'd like some quail for dinner. My father's first question was, "Didn't Cheng set the trap?"

Apparently he had forgotten to set the quail trap, which was a standard operating procedure, and there were no quail available. Cheng's practice was to set the trap, feel the quail, pick out how many fat ones he needed, and turn the rest loose. The next time he needed quail, he'd set the trap a day or so ahead of time, and the quail would accommodate him. On this particular occasion my father said, "Well, Liz, how many do you need?"

My mother answered, "I think about eight. There'll only be you, Frank, and me and Cheng. And, I think Ramon will be here."

So my father said, "Fine, I'd kind of like to go hunting anyway." He got his old shooting jacket, picked up a shotgun, and asked me if I wanted to go along.

I said, "Sure," because I knew the trip would not be too long. We'd go up through the corn patch and come back down along the inside next to the road, following the rail fence which zigzagged between the corn field and the road. The corners in the fence were full of briars and brambles, weeds, and various plants which afforded feed for quail and numerous rabbits, and there were about three coveys that occupied the area along the one fence. The place was usually jumping with cottontails, although they, at that particular time, were not the first order of business. If I remember correctly, my father shot about nine times, ended up with eight quail, and we started home down the road.

About halfway home my father grabbed me and said, "Don't move." I looked up and there, down the road about 100 yards, rearing up, was the biggest bear I have ever seen. I can still feel the cold sweat. That bear got taller and taller as I looked, and I didn't know quite what to do, but I was afraid to move. I heard the shot gun breech open, saw my father make a gesture over each shot gun shell (I couldn't tell quite what he did, but it was so quick it was almost impossible; I finally later figured it out, and of course later he told me) and then they went back into the gun again. Then he looked up and he said, "Mister bear, you big S.O.B., I don't want any part of you, and I'll leave you alone if you leave me alone. Now why don't you just get down off your big high horse and go off some place else."

The bear stood there for a while longer -- he was sitting or standing, or whatever bears do when they rear up and look at you -- and couldn't have been that high, but he looked as if he was at least twelve feet, and he finally went "Rrruuph," and dropped down and started off to the side of the road. I think my father heaved the biggest sigh I've heard in my life. We stood there for another good three or four minutes and he said, "Come on, Frank, let's go home." And we went home.

I later found out that what he had done was to open the shot gun, break out the two shells and cut the casings with his pocket knife where the wad separates the shot from the powder. He was all set then to shoot Mr. Bear with what amounted to two slugs which would have probably kicked the daylights out of him, possibly damaged the shot gun, and seriously hurt my father. But, I think it would have probably finished the bear. Fortunately, that decision didn't have to be made.

One other bear story comes to mind, but I hesitate to tell it because the two versions are so different. My father's version and my uncle's version are the same up to a certain point, and there they part company. It seems that they were on a trip together (where they were going and what they were doing, I have no idea), but they had some pack animals and they were camped on the rim of a small saucer-like valley which was covered with patches of oak brush, shoulder high in places and relatively open in others. The stock had been turned out the night before with a bell mare and only one horse kept in camp. When my father and my uncle woke up in the morning, the bell mare was just across the valley, not very far, and Bill Neal agreed that he would go get her while my father fixed breakfast.

Neal started across the valley and was almost to the stock when my father looked up and saw a bear practically in the middle of the valley. The bear was watching Bill's every move. My father said that if he had shot the bear and wounded him, he knew that he'd take right out after Bill, because he was the object of the bear's attention. My father called to Neal and about that time Neal spotted the bear. The bear watched him for a few minutes and then dropped down and started off in a slightly different direction, angling back toward where my father was located, since that was the easiest way out of the canyon. My father shot him and didn't miss. Neal swore up and down that my father hadn't seen the bear and only shot him to prove what a good marksman he was. My father's version was that if he'd shot the bear while he was watching Neal and then only wounded him, the bear would have torn Bill up, since he had no weapon of any kind. Bill's answer to that was that he had a pocket knife and, by God, he'd have kept whittling at him. I think both of them understood exactly what happened, but to agree was against all the rules of the game, particularly the rules of tall tales. Both of them were very adept in this area.

My father also told a story about a bear which really did him a favor when he was working on the railroad. While it's not really a bear story, the bear is an important actor in the drama that followed. It probably should be designated, "The Story of Brazzle's Dog." Brazzle was my father's harness maker, and this occurred somewhere in Northern Arizona in the course of the work on the Atlantic and Pacific. Good harness makers and good powder men were almost impossible to come by, and one husbanded them like one would a good bottle of wine. Brazzle had a dog. The dog was a big, ugly, mean, rather vicious character who whipped all the other dogs in the camp and was therefore not very popular. My father had given orders to Brazzle to keep his dog tied up at least part of the time, but he never enforced this order -- that is, not too strictly for fear that Brazzle would decide that some other railroad outfit might be a better place to work. My father had a dog, and as long as it was tied up, Brazzle's dog would leave it alone, with the net result that my father's dog was tied up most of the time and Brazzle's had the liberty of the camp.

Somewhere along the line it seemed that rumor had it that a bear was showing up in the evening and going through the garbage pile which was just over the side of the hill, not too far from the cook's shack. The cook had an old needle gun, which is really the grandfather of the present bolt action rifle. The things were about .45 caliber and threw a slug that was pretty good size. When the cook heard about the bear, he immediately cleaned and polished his needle gun and made mighty preparations to take the bear into camp. It seems that one afternoon, just about dusk, someone came running down and told the cook that the bear had been seen at the garbage dump. The cook grabbed his rifle and ran out to look for the bear. Just about that time a large animal skylighted itself on the top of the ridge in the vicinity of the garbage dump. The cook dropped to one knee, took aim, and fired, and he didn't miss. What he shot into practically two pieces was Brazzle's dog.

My father commented afterwards that from then on he didn't have to tie his dog up any longer.

Later I asked my father, "Who alerted the cook?"

He looked at me and chuckled and sort of winked his good right eye and said, "Frank, you know, I'm not sure."

BUSHWHACKER AND DOG STORIES

I often heard my father say that animal intelligence, particularly that possessed by dogs, went considerably beyond the conditioned reflex and memory. Of course, some experiments and observations by Jane Goodall and others have recently indicated that there is considerable credence to this argument. One story in particular that my father used to illustrate this point of view involves a dog that belonged to Walt Cline. Walt managed a ranch about three miles away that was owned by Lon Harmon of Phoenix, and ran the Yolo brand.

It seems that my father and Indian Joe were building a water trough. This was done by taking about a fifteen-foot length of a cedar log, approximately fourteen-inches in diameter, hewing it relatively square on three sides and then digging the fourth side similar to the manner in which dugout canoes are made. This was done by using a large auger, an adz, and an axe. It resulted in a water trough which was watertight. It was relatively light since most of the bulk of the wood had been removed, and would last for a long, long time.

The water trough which they were working on was about one-half completed. One end of it, involving about a third of the length, had been dug to the proper depth. My father said he looked up and here came a dog that belonged to Walt Kline. From his description I can only assume that she was about the size and appearance of a Border Collie and she was carrying a pup in her mouth. She walked over to where they were working, looked around for a moment and put the pup down at Indian Joe's feet and started off. The pup took out after her. He was a little over three weeks old and could waddle along, but he was not too handy. She picked him up and brought him back. He started to follow her again and she repeated the performance. When the pup took after her the third time, she picked him up.

My father said, "Let's see what she'll do."

So both stopped working and the Collie put her pup down inside the water trough at the deep end - it was completely fenced in. My father's comment was "I'll be damned."

With that he saddled up a horse and said to my mother, "I think that old so-and-so that was supposed to be doing the chores at the Cline's has taken off. He's probably left the milk cow, the dog, and a few other animals in a bad way. I'm going to ride over and see what I can do to help out."

Later on in the afternoon he returned, leading a milk cow. Over the horn of the saddle was a flour sack tied together in the middle and at both ends, so it actually made two small bags with two holes cut in the middle. Out of each hole was stuck a pup's head. The Cline's dog had given birth to three pups, and my father was bringing the other two.

Indian Joe was heard to say later, "I hope this cow that Bob brought back from Clines can teach our cow, Lantern, that she can be milked in the daylight and not have to do it after dark." Whether or not this actually happened I don't know, but Indian Joe, Manuel, and Ramon always joked about the fact that the milk cow at the Quarter Circle 81 had to be milked very early in the morning or late at night, due to the fact that if a lantern wasn't used, she'd kick over the milk bucket. Whether this was true or not I don't know, but it was a standing joke.

Another dog story that my father loved to tell should probably be entitled, "The Rumored Mad Dog Story." It seems that he had gone back to Tennessee from Colorado. Exactly why, I don't know, but he indicated that it was to wreak vengeance on some individual who had been a bushwhacker during the Civil War and who had repeatedly robbed my father's family of some of their fine horses.

It seems that in the vicinity of Sweetwater, Tennessee, there lived two brothers, one of whom had a dog which he dearly loved and which the other brother hated with a vengeance. My father was riding down the road, approximately opposite the little farm, when the dog came running out, howling bloody murder. He was followed by one of the brothers, screaming, "Mad dog, mad dog!"

My father said his first reaction was to shoot the dog, and then it suddenly occurred to him that the dog wasn't acting like a mad dog at all, and when the farmer got close enough my father said, "How do you know he's mad?"

The farmer replied, "He's got to be mad, I just pinched his tail in the gate."

Obviously, this brother was not the dog's owner.

My father said he rode on into the area that he called the "knob" which, as near as I can ascertain, are the foothills of the Appalachians. Still looking for the bush-whacker, he met an old minister riding a mule along the side of the road. He stopped him and asked him if he knew where so-and-so lived. The minister replied, "Sure, I know where he lives. Why do you want him?"

My father told him what had happened during the Civil War and said, "I came down here to kill him."

The minister thought for a moment and he said, "Mister, let him live. He's married to old so-and-so and she horsewhips him every Sunday morning. It would be a shame to interrupt that performance."

My father said he thought about it for a while and decided probably that bushwhacker was getting his just dues and he'd leave matters exactly as they were.

The best bushwhacker story was one we called "The Sock Basket Story." This story was told to me by my aunts and uncles. It's been in the family, and I think it's known by many cousins. I was quite amused when Delbert Mann[1] questioned me about it and I found out that his grandmoth-er had told him almost the identical story that my father had told to me.

It seems that during the Civil War the bushwhackers, who were really outlaws or renegades masquerading in either Union or Confederate uniforms, raided the country-side, stealing whatever they could carry off or drive away. They were a real plague to the noncombatants. On one occasion my grandfather had just returned after being rather successful in a poker game. He brought with him a rather substantial sum of money, three or four hundred dol-lars, which was an amazingly large sum at that particular time. My grandmother hid it in a rolled-up sock and tossed

---

[1] *A prolific television, motion picture producer/director who was a cousin and a good friend of my father. [crf]*

it into a sock basket, that is, a basket which was full of socks which needed darning. A knock on the door revealed a number of unlikely soldiers in Union uniforms who my grandmother immediately recognized as renegades. They demanded money and food. She fed them and, in the meantime, they were busy ransacking the house. One of them started in on the sock basket and tossed every pair of undarned socks, each of which was rolled into a ball out on the floor.

When he got to the bottom of the basket, he apparently realized there was nothing left but more sock balls, and he left what amounted to the bottom layer in the basket. He obligingly picked up all the sock balls and put them back in the basket and handed the basket back to my grandmother, who thanked him. After they had gone, everyone gathered around and, sure enough, the sock which held the money was still intact. None of it had been taken, although the bushwhackers had helped themselves to a couple of hams and some bacon which were hanging in the smokehouse.

My father had been out in the hills with the horses, which is why none of those were stolen. It seems that back in Tennessee where he grew up it was his chore to drive the good horses -- and they had half a dozen or so -- out into the hills at night and stay with them until morning. The bushwhacker operation seemed to occur shortly after sundown or just before sunup. They hardly ever approached the homes of apparent noncombatants during the day.

Snipe Hunt at the Caribou Mine

When my father was young he went to work for the Caribou Mine. There were a number of miners there who did not know him and considered him to be somewhat of a greenhorn. They immediately approached him for a snipe hunt. He listened with great interest and asked many questions about the technique of hunting snipe in the Rocky Mountains. How was it done? What was done with the snipe after they were caught? And so forth and so on. A snipe hunt is carried on with a gunny sack, a lantern, and two rocks. The victim is taken out into the woods, given the gunny sack and a lantern, and told to hold the gunny sack open in front of the lantern. When he beats the rocks together, he is told that the snipe (a small bird) will run into the sack. He is then left alone, being told that his friends will be back in half an hour. He is left until he goes home by himself.

It seems that my father had discovered that one of the miners owned a quail net, which probably had been used in the east and middle west to catch bobwhites. It was quite a valuable piece of equipment. According to my father, it was worth twenty or twenty-five dollars in any market. Thus my father encouraged the idea of a snipe hunt, insisting all the time that it would be ideal for him to use the quail net to catch snipe. Since my father showed considerable enthusiasm for the snipe hunt, the miners, particularly the owner of the quail net, fell for this ruse. The owner thus agreed that my father could use the quail net instead of the usual gunnysack.

That night they took my father out and left him holding the lantern behind the quail net. They had no more than gotten out of sight when he took off down to see the store-keeper, whose place of business was about one-half mile down the road, and with whom he'd already made a deal to dispose of the quail net. According to my father, he sold it to the storekeeper for about ten dollars. The snipe hunt was a "howling" success; that is, "howling" as far as the owner of the net was concerned, who never got through complaining about how he'd been taken.

I think my father chuckled over this story for many

years afterwards; I know I heard it at least two or three times, and every time it was good for a twinkle in his eye and a chuckle or two when he visualized the exasperation of the owner of the quail net. "It served him right," he said.

STORIES FROM EARLY PRESCOTT, ARIZONA

In retrospect, Prescott was a series of establishments, commercial in nature, which were important, not only to people who lived there, but to its surrounding environments. In order of importance, they were probably Ruffner's Livery Stable, also known as the Plaza Stable, Garrett's Barber Shop, Murphy's Saloon, the Chinaman's restaurant, Sam Hill's Hardware Store, and M. Goldwater & Bro. dry goods shop. In reverse order, Goldwater's was the place where you bought everything from a cowboy hat to a pair of hand-me-down "Buckingham and Hecht" boots; Hill's was purveyor of horseshoe nails, anvils, iron tires for wagons, guns, and every other hardware item known to man.

Ruffner's Livery Stable was the first important stop for anyone arriving on horseback or driving a team. The freight wagon drivers, after unloading their wares, pulled into Ruffner's to stable their horses through the night. The cowboys, miners, sheepherders and others who rode into town went first to Ruffner's to make sure that their horses were well taken care of. For many of these individuals the next stop was Garrett's. I should say in passing that

Ruffner's performed two functions. That is, the Ruffner family ran the livery stable. Also, one of the Ruffners, from time immemorial seems to always have been the sheriff. There may have been times only one but it always seemed like he was. I was told that he started as Sheriff in the territorial days.

The second stop, as I said before, was Garrett's Barber Shop. Here, you got a bath, a shave, and a haircut. The barber shop was run by the Garrett family, that was, Poppa Garrett and his four sons, all of whom were black and all of whom were highly respected in the community. Louie Lighton, who was a movie producer at Metro-Goldwyn-Mayer, and who at one time had a ranch in Skull Valley, knew the Garrett family and told me later that to get a shave from Poppa Garrett was like having your face caressed with a feather.

All of the prominent citizens in Prescott stopped into Garrett's for a shave before calling on the Chinaman for breakfast. Each had his own shaving mug, and these adorned the north wall, each on its own little shelf. I am certain that the discussions that went on in Garrett's Barber Shop were sufficient to keep the Garrett family fully apprised of everything that was going on, although I never, and I don't think anyone, ever heard of a confidence being violated. On one occasion when I was sitting in the barber shop waiting to get my hair cut, I heard a discussion of politics going on by two other customers seated in chairs. Both of them were getting haircuts, so that they could talk to one another. (If one was getting a shave and covered with a hot, wet towel, conversation was a little difficult.)

The topic was who was going to be the representative to the territorial legislature in Phoenix. Morris Goldwater was one of the parties. He was the head of the Democratic

Prescott, Arizona in 1905

First train into Prescott, Arizona 1887

Parade on Whiskey Row (Montezuma Street) ca 1900.

Whiskey Row as it looked ca 1901, and as it looks today, absent horses, with cars and new shop owners.

Inside M. Goldwater & Bro. clothing store "where you bought everything from a cowboy hat to a pair of hand-me-down 'Buckingham and Hecht' boots" and a lot more.

A parade along Whiskey Row in front of "Sam'l.Hill. Hardware Co." "The purveyor of horseshoe nails, anvils, iron tires for wagons, guns, and every other hardware item known to man." Photograph 1909.

Party, that is, he had been one of the organizers of the Democratic Party in Arizona. The other party to the discussion I remembered as a Republican. The topic of conversation was their respective candidates. The Republican commented to Goldwater that if you sent Goldwater's candidate to the legislature he'd do nothing but play poker which wouldn't do any good for anyone. But, on the other hand, if you sent his candidate to the legislature he wouldn't do anything but work for himself, but in working for himself he'd have to benefit a few others, and therefore he was a better candidate than Goldwater's.

I subsequently found out that the one I had thought was a Republican was a young Democrat named Henry F. Ashurst, who became Arizona's first U.S. Senator in 1912 and who many people remember as a senior and influential senator from Arizona for many years.

It gives you some idea of what went on in Garrett's Barber Shop.

The Chinaman's restaurant was not a Chinese restaurant in the sense that we think of Chinese restaurants today. It was a restaurant run by a Chinaman. The food served was anything but Chinese. You got ham and eggs and buttermilk hotcakes served with honey for breakfast. Dinner, which was served at noon, could be steak and cottage fried potatoes. Supper might be a similar meal, and short orders at other times of the day usually involved some sort of a meat course. Where the Chinaman procured his meat no one really knew. It was good quality. It was unlike most range beef, which is grass fattened, not very tender, and not very palatable compared to the standards that most people today are used to. The Chinaman cooked his steaks, for which he was famous, on a big stove, the top of which was very much like a big hotcake griddle. Places on it were obviously hotter than others, and the Chinaman, who cooked the steaks, knew exactly where the hot spots were. A rare steak was seared on the hottest part on both sides and then cooked for a few seconds on the coolest spot on the top of the stove. It's reputed that a cowboy, having had too many at Murphy's, took one look at one of the Chinaman's rare steaks, jabbed his fork into it, let out a scream, and shouted, "Bawl, damn you, but you can't hook!" There's some question as to whether or not this story is true, but it's still told about the Chinaman.

The fact of the matter was that if you ordered a steak well done, he'd tell you to order a T-bone. That was the only type of steak that could be cooked well done without all of it going up the chimney, according to him. On some occasions when his meat was not the very best, he'd suggest that it probably should be chicken-fried. In this case, the steak was pounded with the claws of a claw hammer, and flour was beaten into it rather thoroughly. It was then cooked rather rapidly in a pan well-greased with tallow and served with a creamed gravy which was made with flour and milk after the steak had been cooked. This went real well with mashed potatoes, which usually accompanied the chicken-fried steak. This type of steak was quite common in cow camps, since cooks could make it in Dutch ovens and it worked very well with the type of meat they were given to work with; that is, grass-fattened beef that was not too well cured. The Chinaman wouldn't approve of this, but when forced to use it he made the best of it.

I can't tell any stories about Murphy's since I was only in the place once. On one occasion my mother was somewhere unavailable and my father was on Montezuma Street. He went in, I think to have a drink, and took me with him -- told the bartender I could use a "soda." The bartender mixed up some concoction which consisted of a flavor of some kind which was unknown to me, some soda water, some sort of simple syrup, and ice. It was the nearest thing to nectar that I had ever tasted. I can't describe it any other way but to say that it was probably the best drink I'd ever had before or since.

THE HANGING OF MURPHY'S KILLER

FOREWORD

The killing and the hanging happened in 1885, long before my Dad was born. The events were reported in the local newspapers.[1] Apparently, a man called Dilda is the fugitive described in the story. After he broke into a neighboring ranch house and stole some "petty articles," the owner swore out a warrant for his arrest. The Deputy Sheriff, John Murphy, went out to arrest him and was shot dead by Dilda. As told in the story, Deputy Sheriff Murphy came by the Ferguson ranch on his way to the house where Dilda was living. According to one of the articles, my grandfather offered to go with deputy Sheriff Murphy, but he didn't think it was necessary. A couple of days later he hadn't come back and my grandfather went to Dilda's house to find him. When he arrived, Dilda told him that if he tried to arrest him he'd kill him. My grandfather then went back and got Sheriff Mulvenon, a posse, some Indian "trailers" and they went after Dilda.

The newspaper clippings are archived at the Sharlot Hall Museum in Prescott, Arizona. An excerpt from the article that describes my grandfather's role follows my Dad's tale, which had been passed down from my grandfather. [crf]

CATCHING THE KILLER

One of the Murphy family usually worked as a deputy Sheriff, and there's quite a story about the Indian trackers. Some renegade committed a

69

crime in Prescott, stole a horse, and headed in a northerly, slightly western direction which would be in the general direction of Camp Wood, but primarily toward the head-waters of Burro Creek. Burro Creek was an area where the Quarter Circle 81 had a horse pasture which consisted of high mesas, mostly rimrock, deep gorges, and a few places which enabled the enclosure of thousands of acres. It was rough, rugged. The country could be extremely dangerous if one didn't know his way about. Murphy, the deputy sheriff, was a knowledgeable lawman who knew the country and knew his business. He had brought in single-hand-edly many criminals considered far more dangerous than the one he was sent after. It was his job to go bring in the renegade, and he took out after him. He stopped at Camp Wood for a change of horses, and when he didn't show up in a couple of days the people at the ranch began to worry. One of the vaqueros was dispatched to Prescott to advise the Sheriff that something must have happened.

Shortly after, two deputies arrived with six Yavapai Indian trackers. It didn't take them very long, after pick-ing up Murphy's tracks at the ranch, to find where the rene-gade had dry-gulched him, stolen his horse, and buried his body in a sand wash. They started after him from there. The Indians were advised that the fugitive was dangerous and if necessary to shoot him on sight. They were armed with single-shot rifles of some ancient vintage, probably comparable to the Martini rifles carried by Kipling's sol-diers in the tales that he tells of India. They were long, octagonal-barreled guns and probably weighed about nine pounds. When the Indians would find a track, one would hold it, and the others would search until they found an overturned pebble or some other indication that the ground had been in some way disturbed. It might be just a broken twig on a bush or a branch knocked off a cactus. They did-n't move rapidly, but they kept on persistently. The trail turned north toward the railroad and, finally into the rough country. The horse that Murphy had ridden was located -- he'd thrown a shoe and turned lame, and the fugitive had turned him loose and was then on foot. The Indians kept on their tracking and after about three days found the man pretending to be asleep under a bush. They ran up with their guns cocked, all ready to fire when the deputy stopped them and said not to shoot him, he'd take care of him. When they searched the renegade, one of them said, "My God, there's Murphy's twenty dollars. I saw the Sheriff give him those two ten-dollar gold pieces when he left."

They brought the man into Prescott and put him in jail. Well, to make a long story short, it didn't take the jury very long to convict the fugitive of murder, and in those days there was no appeal from a criminal conviction.

The verdict was a death sentence and a scaffold was erected in front of the court house in the plaza. This part of the story I know to be true because I was in school at the time of another hanging, and went down to watch them erect the scaffold. Father came down, located me, and took me back up home again, advising me that that wasn't a good place for small boys. It seemed that I was not the only one. Hill's son had gotten the same treatment, so did the Campbell boys and they felt much put out because, after all, their father was a member of the legislature. The men refused to let us witness the hanging, but we heard about it anyway. It seems that justice was done. Penalties were not long delayed by appeals. Punishment was quick and sure.

EPILOGUE

Apparently the last known or reported hanging in Prescott was in 1904. Still, my Dad swears by the fact that he watched a scaffold being built sometime around 1910 in the Plaza at the center of Prescott near where Dilda had been hung. [crf]

The following excerpt is from an article that appeared in a December 1885 Prescott newspaper. It is retyped in its original form for legibility.

DOOMED DILDA'S DEED

His Cowardly Assassination of Deputy Sheriff John M. Murphy.

Since our last issue this community has been thrown into a state of melancholy feeling intermingled only now and then by lust for revenge on the perpetrators of a series of crimes which, to our recollection, is only equalled in atrocity by the dastardly deeds of the notorious Bender family. The victims of the heinous crimes were our efficient and popular Deputy Sheriff John M. Murphy; and a man named James Jenkins, and later reports have created the belief that still another man has suffered the same fate of these two by being foully murdered by a cold blooded coward named Dilda, assisted by his equally brutal wife, at Walnut Creek, about 37 miles from Prescott.

Dilda had been employed by Mr. W. H. Williscraft, a prominent stockman of this county, to take charge of his ranch at Walnut Creek a few months since, but it was only a short time until Mr. Williscraft discovered he had a decidedly undesirable occupant of his premises. Adjoining the ranch where Dilda lived Mr. Williscraft owned another place, which Dilda broke into and stole a few petty articles. Mr. Williscraft thinking this a good opportunity to rid himself of the unpleasant neighbor swore out a warrant against him for petty larceny. The warrant was placed in the hands of John Murphy, who proceeded to Walnut Creek to serve the same. On the way out he met P. J. McCormick, who warned him of the dangerous character with whom he had to deal, but with his usual coolness went on to within about a mile and a half of Dilda's place, where he left his horse and proceeded on foot. He reached Dilda's house and found only his wife and child in, who informed him that Dilda had gone out. After searching the premises thoroughly for his man he retraced his steps to the ranch of Mr. Behm's, where he waited until night. After refusing proffered assistance about 8 o'clock he again started for his man and this was the last seen of him alive.

Mr. Williscraft hearing some shots fired about 9 o'clock, jumped on his horse and rode up near the scene and whistled, to which someone quickly responded, and in a few minutes he noticed a man about 150 yards distant creeping toward him. Wisely fearing that he would soon receive a bullet he dismounted, and using his horse as a shield drew off. The next morning he drove up to Dilda's stable and went in, and in a few minutes noticed a gun leveled at him in the hands of Dilda, and quickly jumped behind a wagon. At this moment Mr. Ferguson came up, and Dilda informed them that he would kill any man who came to arrest him. Looking around, Mr. Ferguson soon discovered tracks indicating that a dead body had been dragged a short distance and then picked up and carried off. Jumping at the right conclusion, he quickly mounted a horse and brought the news of Murphy's death to town.

Sheriff Mulvenon and posse were soon en route to the scene and on arrival there found the report too true, as Murphy's remains had already been dug up from the cellar, where he had been buried in a sack.

In the meantime Dilda had escaped and was on his way

Dilda, his wife and children

out of the country. Sheriff Mulvenon and posse were soon on the trail, which was followed to Ash Fork. At this point the posse was reinforced, and as Dilda was seen there a short time previous his escape was impossible. In a short time he was found about two miles from Ash Fork, where he was stretched out for a sleep. He was told to throw up his hands, which command he complied with as soon as looking up. It was only by the strong appeal by Sheriff Mulvenon that the posse allowed the prisoner to be brought here and placed in jail.

Since his confinement in jail investigation has unearthed another horrible murder....

The article as it appeared in the December 1885, Prescott newspaper. The underlining was added after this photocopy was made.

DOOMED DILDA'S DEED.

His Cowardly Assassination of Deputy Sheriff John M. Murphy.

Since our last issue this community has been thrown into a state of melancholy feeling intermingled only now and then by lust for revenge on the perpetrators of a series of crimes which, to our recollection, is only equalled in atrocity by the dastardly deeds of the notorious Bender family. The victims of the hienous crimes were our efficient and popular Deputy Sheriff John M. Murphy, and a man named James Jenkins, and later reports have created the belief that still another man has suffered the same fate of these two by being foully murdered by a cold blooded coward named Dilda, assisted by his equally brutal wife, at Walnut Creek, about 37 miles from Prescott.

Dilda had been employed by Mr. W. H. Williscraft, a prominent stockman of this county, to take charge of his ranch at Walnut Creek a few months since, but it was only a short time until Mr. Williscraft discovered he had a decidedly undesirable occupant of his premises. Adjoining the ranch where Dilda lived Mr. Williscraft owned another place, which Dilda broke into and stole a few petty articles. Mr. Williscraft thinking this a good opportunity to rid himself of the unpleasant neighbor swore out a warrant against him for petty larceny. The warrant was placed in the hands of John Murphy, who proceeded to Walnut Creek to serve the same. On the way out he met P. J. McCormick, who warned him of the dangerous character with whom he had to deal, but with his usual coolness went on to within about a mile and a half of Dilda's place, where he left his horse and proceeded on foot. He reached Dilda's house and found only his wife and child in, who informed him that Dilda had gone out. After searching the premises thoroughly for his man he retraced his steps to the ranch of Mr. Behm's, where he waited until night. After refusing proffered assistance about 8 o'clock he again started for his man and this was the last seen of him alive.

Mr. Williscraft hearing some shots fired about 9 o'clock jumped on his horse and rode up near the scene and whistled, to which some one quickly responded, and in a few minutes he noticed a man about 150 yards distant creeping toward him. Wisely fearing that he would soon receive a bullet he dismounted, and using his horse as a shield drew off. The next morning he drove up to Dilda's stable and went in, and in a few minutes noticed a gun leveled at him in the hands of Dilda, and quickly jumped behind a wagon. At this moment Mr. Ferguson came up, and Dilda informed them that he would kill any man who come to arrest him. Looking around Mr. Ferguson soon discovered tracks that indicated that a dead body had been dragged a short distance and then picked up and carried off. Jumping at the right conclusion he quickly mounted a horse and brought the news of Murphy's death to town.

Sheriff Mulvenon and posse were soon en route to the scene, and on arrival there found the report too true, as Murphy's remains had already been dug up from the cellar, where he had been buried in a sack.

In the meantime Dilda had escaped and was on his way out of the country. Sheriff Mulvenon and posse were soon on the trail, which was followed to Ash Fork. At this point the posse was reenforced, and as Dilda was seen there a short time previous his escape was impossible. In a short time he was found about two miles from Ash Fork, where he was stretched out for a sleep. He was told to throw up his hands, which command he complied with as soon as looking up. It was only by the strong appeal made by Sheriff Mulvenon that the posse allowed the prisoner to be brought here and placed in jail.

Since his confinement in jail investigation has unearthed another horrible murder. A short time since Mr. Williscraft hired a man named Jenkins at Ash Fork to assist Dilda on the ranch, and upon going to the ranch and finding Jenkins missing, enquired of Dilda where he was. Dilda informed him that Jenkins complained of being sick and went to Prescott to the hospital. Search failing to find him here created stronger suspicion that he had been murdered as it was supposed he was possessed of some money. The tracks of a man and woman following a wheelbarrow from Dilda's house was discovered, and this trail was followed for about one hundred yards to the point where it stopped. Under about two feet of earth and rocks the ghastly remains of Jenkins were discovered.

The prisoners are both of slight build and in the neighborhood of thirty years of age. Although not desperate characters in appearance, the coolness with which they view the situation indicates their cold-blooded nature. It is said that Dilda has left a trail of blood behind him in Texas, from whence he came to the Salt river valley two years ago. If the woman's tale is to be believed she is not as deep in the mire as was at one time supposed. We learn since the above was in type that she has made a confession to the grand jury, in which her husband alone is implicated in the murders.

Johnnie Murphy had a multitude of friends among the stockmen of this county, many of whom followed the remains to town, where a large meeting was held by citizens to consider the question of restitution. Wiser counsel prevailed, however, and the law was allowed to deal justice provided it took action quickly. The remains of John M. Murphy were sadly laid to rest on Thursday, followed to the grave by the largest procession of solemn mourners ever seen in Prescott.

The Grand Jury brought in an indictment for murder against Dilda and he will be arraigned on Monday, when he will plead not guilty, and it is understood will make the ridiculous defense that Mr. Williscraft committed the murder. As all the evidence will prove conclusively that Dilda committed the deed, it is not probable that it will be a great while before the many friends of Johnnie Murphy will witness the execution of his assassin on the plaza at Prescott.

This morning Dilda sent for Judge E. M. Sanford for consultation. The Judge went over to the cell and Dilda represented that he owned land near Phenix worth $2,000, which he would turn over as a fee. Mr. Sanford consented to be appointed by the court for the purpose of arraignment and in the meantime wired Phenix to know how the land lay, and received an answer saying that Dilda had no property; that the land jumped by him was owned by Joe Reed. Mr. Sanford at once declined to have anything further to do with the case.

Sharlot Hall Museum,
Prescott, Arizona

77

MORE ABOUT CATTLE - LONGHORNS TO HEREFORDS

The cattle originally at the Quarter Circle 81 were primarily longhorns, salted and peppered with a few Mexican cattle that came into Arizona, probably from California or from Old Mexico. The Mexican cattle were sort of chocolate-colored. Their horns were shorter than longhorns and stuck out at almost a right angle from their heads. They were, by normal standards, about as rough as the longhorns, but somewhat smaller and boxier and, consequently, were probably better beef cattle. An example of Mexican cattle appeared a short time ago in a commercial aired by Merrill Lynch with a voiceover that "Merrill Lynch is bullish on America." What was shown was a herd of cattle which were a fine example of what has been standard Mexican cattle for at least ninety years. I guess, after all, Merrill Lynch is bullish on America -- if not all of America, at least North America. Both of these types, longhorns and Mexican cattle, were materially improved by selective breeding.

Somewhere along the line my father acquired a number of muley bulls, that is, bulls without horns. They were parti-colored, shorter-legged, and actually better beef cattle than the longhorns. They were also predominant insofar as throwing the muley characteristics was concerned. Many of the calves from cows with horns were muleys, and the bull calves were retained and eventually replaced many of the horned bulls that were initially part of the herd. Strange as it may seem, the muley bulls, given near equal size and experience, were superior fighters when it came to defending their territories around water holes. It wasn't very long until the better areas were dominated by muley bulls. This, of course, resulted in many more muley calves.

Somewhere along the line, Manuel Altaininano suggested that certain cows seemed to be having calves that grew faster and were healthier than others and that these cows used certain water holes. From this he reasoned that possibly the bulls who dominated these particular water holes had something to do with the size and weight-gaining factors of the calves. Ramon doubted this theory. My father wasn't sure if it had any real validity, and I remember hearing him discussing it with my mother and suggesting that it was impossible in the absence of the ability to weigh the calves breed the same cows to different bulls, and then weigh those calves to determine whether or not there was any soundness to the theory. Nevertheless, he let Manuel determine which bulls we would eliminate if the choice between two occurred. Subsequent experiments at the University of Texas proved that one of the main factors in the weight gain is based on the bulls. So actually Manuel was not far from the mark. What this young cowpuncher had observed turned out to be scientifically correct. With him it was just a guess, at best a theory. But, with the University of Texas it was a scientifically proved fact.

About 1908 or 1909 my father made a deal with someone, I don't know who, to import about ten or twelve Hereford bulls. These were not purebreds, but they were good stock and they were dark red, whitefaced, and boxed like the Herefords recognized at the present time. This resulted, of course, in disenfranchising a lot of bulls that had occupied the territory before. When the new Herefords took over they were actually excellent browsers and hustlers as far as their feed was concerned, and did well on the grama grass and oak brush browse range. The first bunch of calves were what is known as motley faces. In other words, they weren't whitefaced like good Herefords, but their faces were red and white spotted or red and white splotched. The second generation, however, bred to motley faced heifers, produced whitefaced calves that showed many of the Hereford characteristics. These cattle brought a much higher price on the market than those that had been marketed prior to the introduction of the Hereford bulls. When this experiment was first undertaken by my father, many of the cattlemen thought he was crazy and that the longhorn and muley bulls on the range would keep the little Herefords from the water holes, and they would end up being surplus. But due to careful management and control of who was where, or I should say, which bulls were where, the experiment worked beautifully.

The prices for Quarter Circle 81 cattle went up materially in the market. In retrospect it seems clear that the longhorns were bred primarily to travel. That is, from Texas to the railroad heads and into Montana, Wyoming, and other parts of the West where the big ranches were stocked with cattle that came out of Texas. In other words, the beef factor or food factor was secondary. Traveling was the primary purpose for which these cattle were raised. This was not true of the Herefords. When my father started crossing the Herefords with the cattle that were on the Arizona range at that time, he actually started breeding real beef cattle as distinguished from crosses whose forebears had been pilgrims rather than T-bone steaks.

A TRUE STORY OF HASSAYAMPA RIVER

One of the legends predominant in Arizona was the legend of the Hassayampa River. If you ever drank its water you could never tell the truth again, at least so the story went. Every miner, every cowpuncher, every section hand who worked on the railroad which crossed the river, every bar janitor, and everyone else who ever wandered around and told tales, had his own story as to how he had been prevented or escaped the tragedy of drinking that tainted water. I've always thought that Ed did about as good a job on this legend as anyone I ever heard. According to Ed, he and his horse were crossing the dry desert-like area which existed on one side of the river. Ed had planned to get water at a water hole that he knew about prior to reaching the river. When he reached the water hole he found that it was filled with mud, fouled by burros, and absolutely undrinkable. There was nothing to do but go on to the river. By the time he reached the river he was walking, almost crawling, and leading his horse, which was also in a state of total exhaustion. When they had reached the river the horse shoved his nose into the water clear up to his eyeballs and drank his fill. Ed debated for

The Hassayampa River ca 1882.

a long time and decided he had to take the chance. He reached down and scooped up his hat full of water. As everyone knows, every cowboy and vaquero has fed his horse using his hat to hold a little bit of grain as a substitute for a nose bag. Ed was just rinsing off his hat. The horse finished drinking, and slammed his nose into Ed's hat, thinking it was full of oats and knocked the hat out of Ed's hand and into the river. Ed fell into the water, recovered his hat, but didn't drink any water according to him.

When he reached the bank he was sufficiently refreshed to climb on the horse, which had recovered from his dried-out condition, and he was able to carry Ed on to a spring where the water was not tainted as was the Hassayampa. At this point Ed usually stopped and waited. Someone always asked the pertinent question, "What about the horse, Ed?"

He always smiled slightly and said, "I don 't know, he never talked to me about it."

THE ELK/GIRAFFE-
LIKE CATTLE

At one time rumors began to circulate around Prescott about a strange animal down in Skull Valley. It was long-legged like an elk, had a long neck almost like a giraffe, was tall as a horse, and had a face like a horse, except its upper lip was like a monkey. The Indians described it in some detail. When one of them was asked what its tracks looked like, he threw up his hands and was unable even to draw anything like a picture of a track in the dust. Rumors kept coming in about this strange animal. Most of them were from the Yavapai Indians who, of course, at one time had used the Hassayampa River as their water source. Consequently, their statements were somewhat suspect. It was also believed by many that the Yavapai told tall tales just to confuse the Anglos. They had many stories about rich dry placers, gold lodes, silver deposits, and large herds of beautiful mustang horses.

Searching never found any of them. No one ever found the horses or located any of the mines, so the stories about this strange animal were subject to many doubts. The inability of the Indians, however, to draw the hoof print created a real problem since the hoof print or foot print would give a real clue as to the animal's nature. The more this animal was described the more certain people, particularly the Yavapai County Librarian, decided that it must be a camel. She showed a picture of a camel to an Indian and he looked at it for a long time. Finally shook his head and said, "No, that wasn't it." Then he came back and asked to see the picture again and studied it again. He again told the librarian that that wasn't what he had seen in Skull Valley.

Two cowpokes, after a couple of drinks in Murphy's Saloon, decided to ride out and see just exactly what this animal was. And, sure enough, it didn't take them very long to locate it. It was a camel. It was one of the camels that had been brought over here from Africa by the army and it was part of the "camel corps" they had used in the southwest desert. It had been turned loose or gotten away and wandered almost two hundred miles from where it had originally been in service. How it managed to do this is quite unknown. But nevertheless, there it was. And then the question arose, how come the Indian, after having seen a picture of the camel, was unable to identify it as such? And the mystery was solved. The picture that the librarian had showed the Indian was a picture of an Asian camel, not an African camel. The picture he saw had two humps. The camel in Skull Valley only had one. The mystery, after all, was solved; it was an African camel.

FRIENDSHIPS

Camp Wood was quite famous as a place for wild game. There were quail in the little valley and many deer in the surrounding areas. Every fall some of my father's friends came out on a deer hunt. They always drove out to Camp Wood in a wagon and were more than welcome to stay at the ranch house. However, they never did. They always camped at a little spring which was across the road from the corral and which had been fenced and then logged up so that the water was channeled down into a series of troughs a considerable distance below where the spring came out of the rocks.

This situation made an ideal camp spot. Hill the hardware merchant, Murphy the saloon keeper, Ron Harmon, a banker from Phoenix, and a Catholic priest whose name I don't know were camped there on one occasion. My father asked me if I wanted to go over with him to visit with them. Of course I went along. When we got there the deer were strung up, cleaned but not skinned (hung out to cool at night) and there were four hunters. The saloon keeper was getting ready to fry a deer liver. The priest was rolling out a batch of biscuits to bake in a Dutch oven which he had heating in the fire and he was using a quart bottle half full of whiskey for a rolling pin. This, of course, had been Murphy's contribution.

My father said, "I see three of you have been successful, who's short?"

Murphy said, "I'm short, and if I don't get a deer tomorrow I'm going to cuss a little bit."

The priest said, "Well, if you think it will help, go ahead. After all, maybe somebody will hear you and if it's the right guy probably you'll get a good shot."

Actually, the next day Murphy brought in a four-point buck that was a beauty. Whether he cussed a little bit ahead of time we never found out.

One thing is certain, the camaraderie among the oldtimers in Prescott and the tolerance and understanding with which they treated one another was actually a phase of civilization which I think is sadly lacking in mankind at the present time. It's really too bad that we can't treat one another with the courtesy, the respect, and the affection with which those oldtimers, those pioneers, dealt with one another.

THE EARLY
CHINESE SETTLERS

The Chinaman who ran the restaurant in Prescott was not the only Chinese there. Prescott had a sizable Chinese population who lived on the north end of Granite Street, which was the area north of Goodwin Street. Granite Street south of Goodwin Street was known as the tenderloin or red light district. The Chinese worked in many of the homes as cooks and servants. They ran a number of laundries and they performed other services of one kind or another. The laundries turned out beautiful work, and most of the shirts worn by the gentry in Prescott were done up by the Chinamen. The housewives, however, considered the techniques of the Chinese to be decidedly off limits. Every Chinese laundryman ironed clothes with a real hot iron, and sprinkled them in a manner which was unique to Chinese. It seemed to be a custom utilized by them all over the West. By some technique they were able to take a mouthful of water, purse their lips in such a manner as to emit a fine spray over the garment to be ironed. The process was much better than could be done by hand, as was done by the usual laundress. Spitting on

Chinese Parade ca 1900

clothes was a common Chinese custom, at least that was the way the practice was described by those who disapproved.

The Chinese continued to wear their pigtails and most of them dressed in a Chinese costume which looked like a pair of pajamas made of a cloth about the color of bleached denim. What the cloth was actually made of I don't know, but I think it was a cotton of some kind or another. On formal occasions this light blue costume was changed to jet black.

Jet black was worn in connection with Chinese funerals. When a Chinaman died, I think all of Chinatown turned out in mourning. The parade which followed the hearse out Gurley Street was blocks long. The funeral was celebrated by the lighting of many firecrackers. These were the little Chinese firecrackers that we called ladyfingers. The Chinese fired them by lighting one fuse that lighted the whole package rather than lighting them individually the way the small boys did with the larger firecrackers that they shot off during the Fourth of July. In addition to the firecrackers, the Chinamen scattered strips of paper about the width of an adding machine tape and about six inches long all the way along the line of march. Each one of these papers was perforated with a jillion holes, and each Chinaman had a bag full of these things, with the net result that it took the street cleaners days to clean up Gurley Street after a Chinese funeral. Just what the purpose of the papers were no one ever seemed to be sure, but rumor had it that the Chinese believed that the evil spirits had to go through each one of the holes in each one of the pieces of paper before they could get to the spirit of the dead. This would give the spirit plenty of time to depart from this earth and to end up wherever it was good to end up. I don't know whether this is true or not, but anyway it's a pretty good explanation and it sort of answers the question.

On the Fourth of July we usually had firecrackers that were probably made in China, which were much larger than the Chinese firecrackers, and which we separated and fired one by one. If you separated the ladyfingers, only about half of them seemed to explode. When I was in the first grade I mentioned this to a friend of mine, a Chinese boy, and he explained to me that the Chinese firecrackers were not supposed to be separated but were to be fired or exploded in bunches, and that the only way to do this was to light the main fuse and not separate them. This way, for some odd reason, they all exploded; and he was correct, they did. Why this worked out the way it did I'm not certain, but anyway, that was the technique that we used from then on.

INDIAN JOE
AND CHENG

I am not sure, but I believe Indian Joe and Cheng came to work for my mother and father when my mother was running the stage stop station. Joe took care of the chores, milked the cows, cut the wood, and did the odd jobs which were necessary in an operation such as hers. Cheng was the cook. Between the two of them they also managed to grow a garden of considerable proportions south of the house. They rock-dammed the creek and diverted part of it so that the needed water could be used for irrigation. The rock dam was partially destroyed during the winter flood periods so that the stream stayed in its course and didn't overflow into the area used for the garden.

The produce was mostly used at the ranch. But I believe some of it was also sold to the people at the Hillside Mine because I have heard my mother talk about sacking cabbage, three heads to a gunny sack, to ship to the Hillside mine. Cheng, of course, was at the height of his glory when he had all the fresh vegetables that he wanted to use. His technique for cooking cabbage and carrots and even turnips made all three of them very palatable. And the sweet corn that was raised was excellent. Always there were a couple of rows of popcorn which were harvested or shucked, and some of it saved for Christmas tree decorations. There was always considerable conversation that it would get too hot and the corn would pop during the fall. But of course, this was pure speculation, pure hokum, and it never happened. But nevertheless, it caused me considerable concern.

I think Joe came from the Haulapai tribe (spelled either Walapai or Haulapai, I believe either version is acceptable, and I think the present maps show the H beginning preferable although it's still sounded as a W regardless of which spelling is used). The Hualapai reservation is north and somewhat east of Kingman. The Hualapai at the present time carry on the business of servicing the raft trips that come down the Colorado River. They charge for camp sites and they also furnish some provisions for the rafters who have had a little difficulty and lost some of their supplies. The Hualapais, unlike the Yavapais, were good husbanders of their land -- they raised good horses, they had some cattle and a reputation for being relatively reliable.

Where Joe learned to make bridle conchas and to braid riatas, to make spurs and to inlay them, I have no idea, but he was excellent. His headstalls for bridles, which were also braided four round, were much in demand.

Cheng was a small Cantonese. He was about five feet six inches tall and his costume was the usual Chinese pajamas, plus a white apron. The apron was actually not an apron at all; it was a flour sack which had been taken apart and washed until the sizing was out of it, which he then tucked in some way or another around the top of his pants. He bossed my mother around as if he were the owner of the ranch instead of one of the hired hands, and I doubt very much if anyone could have fired him. He had an attitude of proprietorship that only the landed gentry would normally exhibit, and some of his practices were unbelievable. He never carried in a bucket of water from the well. He always managed to get someone else to do it. Just how he handled this I was never quite sure, but it always seemed that when the water bucket was empty, Joe or Manuel or Ramon or even my Dad went out and ran the bucket down into the well, hoisted it out full of water, and brought it back into the kitchen.

Cheng's clothes-sprinkling technique was the same as all the other Chinese. My mother frowned on this, but she couldn't prevent him from at least ironing his own clothes, even though she wouldn't always let him iron anything that she had anything to do with. Cheng had another practice that always amused me. I never saw him get caught at it, but whenever my mother wasn't watching him and he had a steak to fry, he always spit in the frying pan to see whether it was hot enough or not. If the spit bounced out, it was; if it didn't bounce out he heated it some more. This sounds pretty unhygienic but, if you stop and think about it, the heat from the stove sterilized the pan, and it was probably just as safe as if he'd behaved himself.

Cheng didn't cut off his pigtail until long after the other Chinamen in Prescott had done away with theirs, which I think came shortly after the Boxer Rebellion. His one grand desire was that he eventually be sent back to China when he died. I can't even guess as to how old he was; he looked the same from the time I first remember him until the last time I saw him in about 1912. He was one of those Orientals that aged up to a point, and then looked the same for the next fifty years.

He was a poker player deluxe, and no one at the ranch would ever play poker with him. The danger was that he would not only win all your money, but he'd win all your paraphernalia, including your horse, if you'd bet it with him. Whenever a drifter stopped by for a free meal he was always warned not to play poker with Cheng. If he made the mistake and ended up on foot, that was his fault. It didn't happen very often, but every once in a while somebody would decide he could take the Chinaman into camp, and that was one of the big mistakes of his life. Cheng was also very good at cribbage, and he used to play pinochle with my mother. She could beat him occasionally. When she did he wailed and carried on as if somebody had cut his heart out.

Cheng was quite profane and his profanity, coupled with a Chinese accent, was really amusing. Unbeknownst to everyone else, I used to imitate him.

One time when I was playing, doing something under the dining room table, Cheng knocked off a ball of beeswax that he was using on some thread to sew something together, his leather belt or one of his shoes or some other piece of paraphernalia. It came tumbling down and landed right square on top of my head. I jumped up and called Cheng all his own favorite Chinese names, with all the little fancy side dressings that were typically Chinese, only to realize that my mother was standing in the doorway between the dining room and the living room. I had no place to retreat, I had no excuse, and I had no defense. The result was that I got worked over with the wooden side of a hairbrush, forcibly and effectively. It was amazing, after that, how I cleaned up my act. I don't think I ever imitated Cheng again, at least not where anybody could hear me.

There were two dishes that I remember that Cheng cooked that I believe were his own invention, or else my mother taught him.

The first was cabbage, which he chopped up very finely in a chopping bowl. He put a little bacon grease in the frying pan, dumped in the cabbage, added about three or four tablespoons of water, salt and pepper, and put a lid on it. He cooked this for a very short period of time and sort of steamed it. The cabbage came out with a flavor and texture that is nothing quite like anything I have ever tasted before, and it's one of the few methods of cooking cabbage which I think makes the vegetable palatable. He even did it this way when he served it with corned beef, which was a common dish at the ranch. He put the beef down in the brine, it was one of the ways of keeping it.

Another dish was carrots. Cheng contended that the average method produced nothing but rabbit food. He cut the carrots into thin slices and served them in a cream sauce. How he made the cream sauce I don't know, because I've never tasted anything quite like it. But here again was a mouth-watering dish if I've ever encountered one. I've often thought I'd like to try and figure out how he did it. I've tried a half a dozen different methods but never even come close.

CHENG'S CONTRIBUTION TO THE RIGHT-TO-WORK LAWS

In 1909 my mother and I moved to Prescott so that I could attend kindergarten. Kindergarten in Prescott at that time was for four- and five-year-olds. I qualified on two grounds: I was four years old in September, and I would be five in November. We lived in a house on Union Street, a street a block south of Gurley on the hilltop in back of the Murphy house. It was about four to five minutes' walk down the hill to Washington School, which was on Gurley Street. There were three other boys who lived in the same block: Art Harkins, who lived next door, and the two Campbell boys, whose father was in the legislature, who lived down at the corner to the east. Art Harkin took me to class and introduced me to some of the other children at school. It was here that I learned about marbles, that is, doe-babes, glassies, steelies, stonies and the highly prized agates. We weren't supposed to play for keeps but everyone did, and it wasn't long before I learned the value of doe-babes as compared to glassies, the highly-prized agates, and the steelies, which were really just oversized ball bearings, and stonies, which were good shooters. Stonies and agates both tended to stick in the spot where the other marble was knocked out, which was a great advantage in a game called little ring.

It was during about the third week of school that I caught the measles. There was an epidemic in Prescott, and I wasn't the only small boy that had them. It turned out that my mother had never had the measles either, and she caught them from me. She was very ill, and for a short time we were taken care of by a member of the Garrett family -- one of the daughters who came in and helped out. Eventually, some of her family also became ill and she had to help at home. We were in rather a difficult situation. My mother wrote a letter to the ranch, which Art Harkin mailed, and it wasn't long until my father showed up with Cheng. Cheng came prepared to stay awhile. He had a small sort of carpetbag for his clothes and the piece of culinary equipment which he used for all purposes. This item was sort of like a butcher's cleaver, only square. The blade, instead of being wedge-shaped like a cleaver, was honed to an edge like a butcher knife. He could peal a potato, shave a water chestnut, trim a steak, or do most any other thing with it that required an instrument with a sharp edge. With this instrument he was a master, and he was never without it. He proceeded to tell my mother that he would take care of things and that she needn't worry about anything. It wasn't very long until he was real busy doing the washing, the ironing, haggling with the hucksters, doing what marketing there was to be done, and cooking broths and soups and delicate meals for my mother. For some unknown reason, the soup I seemed to get about 90 percent of the time was oyster stew, made with a very high grade of canned oysters, but nevertheless oyster stew. I've never been able to look it in the face since.

Cheng cleaned the house, dusted the furniture, did everything from being chief cook and bottle washer to parlor maid and head nurse in the bargain. He bossed my mother around unmercifully, insisted that she remain carefully in bed and keep the blinds drawn so that the light would not affect her eyes, since it was rumored that bright light was bad for measles patients. He moved me from my bedroom into a small room that had been a storage room which was closer to my mother's bedroom so, according to Cheng, he could better take care of me. He also insisted that my room remain darkened and that the instructions left by Dr. Yount be meticulously followed. Cheng was probably a better head nurse than any woman I have ever encountered in my numerous journeys to various hospitals in Los Angeles.

It seems that about the time that Cheng was taking care of my mother and me, the labor union which was then known as the Wobblies or the IWW, or possibly the ALU, was engaged in organizing the copper miners at Jerome and the gold miners at Crown King. Someone got the bright idea that the domestics in Prescott should be unionized. The domestic workers in Prescott were predominantly Chinese who, like Cheng, were very loyal to the people for whom they had worked for many years. There were some Hispanics, and there were a few blacks. Most of these people had been with their families for many years and were really more like family than like servants. The union organizers in those days were referred to as walking delegates. When the walking delegate showed up in Prescott he ran into some resistance from a number of the people whom he contacted and he was not too successful.

The local paper, *The Prescott Journal Miner*, had a few

editorial comments on these efforts, none of which were very encouraging. It seems that the walking delegate -- I have no idea whether he was ALU, which was "One Big Union," or whether he was an IWW delegate -- called on Cheng. My mother tells of her hearing this altercation in the back of the house, or on the back porch, she's not sure which, which sounded like an argument and then a series of loud screams which obviously came from Cheng, coupled with some of his own prized profanity. The next thing she noticed was the walking delegate running pell-mell down the side of the house between the house and the fence to get to the street. He turned the corner with Cheng right after him, his pigtail standing out behind, his cleaver in his hand, waving it, and he was in full cry. The last that was seen of either of them, on that particular morning, was the delegate running down the hill toward Goldwater's Dry Goods Store which was on the corner of Cortez and the Union street where we lived.

After a while, Cheng returned announcing that he had repelled all boarders and that everything was under control. A short while later the news seems to have gotten around that there had been a footrace run down the hill toward Goldwater's dry good store and the Chinaman had come in second. The Journal Miner, in the next issue (it was a weekly paper) raised some question as to what had happened to the efforts to unionize the Prescott domestics; that no efforts had been observed during the last few days.

My father, upon learning of the incident later when he came to visit us, had a number of rather amusing remarks. First, what if Cheng could have actually caught the delegate? Second, what if he really wanted to catch him? Some time later he finally resolved this dilemma by deciding that Cheng had about as much chance of catching him as a celluloid cat had of survival after being chased by an asbestos dog through hell.

MORE THAN
ENOUGH JERKY

One year, after my family had moved to Prescott, I think we went on to Los Angeles and returned to the Quarter Circle 81 about the middle of September. Only Joe and Cheng were there, and Cheng was beside himself. You would have thought he had been on a starvation diet for weeks. There was no more salt pork, an essential with which to cook pinto beans; he was down to his last side of bacon, and there was no doubt that he and Joe were in great danger of starving to death although, as my father pointed out, there was plenty of flour and other staples, and there were still many vegetables available in the garden, and new potatoes and peas were readily available. But what Cheng really wanted was a beef killed, and he went through all sorts of vocal gyrations to accomplish this end. My father finally suggested, I think in desperation, that Ed should endeavor to kill a deer, preferably a forked horn or a three pointer, not a large one, since it was really too early in the year to hang out meat very effectively and keep it for any long period of time. And the acquisition of a small buck would solve the problem. This, to Joe, appeared to present no problem, since he kept rather careful track of the deer herds and where they were; although he indicated that the big bucks were probably still high in the hills, he didn't think that he would have too much difficulty.

The first day provided no results. The second was similar although, to give Joe his just due, he was actually digging up water holes and putting out salt along with his deer hunting activities, so he probably couldn't concentrate. Nevertheless, the third day turned up with a similar result.

About this time Manuel and Ramón arrived from a sojourn to Prescott, or some other place where they had been, and undertook to augment the hunting activity. The three hunters returned empty handed. The next day the same result occurred. The third time the three of them were out, there was still no product.

My father finally decided that if nothing happened the next day by noon, he'd kill a beef. Noon arrived and he and Cheng slaughtered a motley faced Hereford heifer, about a two-year-old. They had just finished skinning it when Joe arrived and advised that he needed a pack horse to bring in a buck that he had just killed. It wasn't over half an hour until the same process was repeated. Manuel had been successful, so had Ramón. There we were with three deer and a two-year-old. That was more meat than anyone needed. There wasn't anything to do with it except jerk it.

The next morning, Cheng advanced on the blacksmith's shop where the grindstone was located, with an armload of butcher knives (all manufactured by Bishop in Manchester, England), and proceeded to put a sharp edge on every one of them. Then all the hands set to work. Ramón swears up and down to this day that he strung at least a quarter of a mile of bailing wire on which to hang the jerky. It was all over the place. My mother claimed the whole back yard was useless to hang out the laundry for a full four days. Fortunately, the Yolo was able to take some of it off our hands, so did the people at the Pitchfork. So actually we ended up with a season's supply of jerky, all acquired practically over a weekend.

SELLING CATTLE - THE CAMP WOOD CATTLE DRIVE

(With a little Sheep Dip)

To get the cattle from Camp Wood to market it was necessary to drive them to the railroad. This meant to a shipping point which was either Hackberry or Seligman on the Santa Fe which crosses Arizona from Needles, through Kingman, and on across to Holbrook. The drive from Camp Wood was about fifty miles, maybe a little more. It took about five days to get there and about two to come home. The ranches in the area usually combined. In other words, the Yolo, the Pitchfork, the Quarter Circle 81, and sometimes the Cross Triangle all drove their cattle in one drive or in one bunch from the Williamson Valley area to the shipping point. This was an easy drive compared to the drives of the Texas cattle. It was taken slowly, and by combining forces there were plenty of men to handle the herd. At the shipping point the cattle were weighed. If they had already been purchased by a buyer who had examined them on the range and bought them on the per-animal basis, for instance for thirty, forty, and fifty dollars a head for one-, two-, and three-year-old steers, the cattle were not weighed; they were merely prodded into stock cars and shipped to a destination somewhere in the Midwest where they went into feed lots.

Unlike the Texas drives, gear was carried on pack animals. (This included not only the cook's paraphernalia but also the blanket rolls of the various cowpunchers).

On one occasion I remember my father came home from the drive, which I think had taken him to Hackberry, walked into the house looking a little bit sheepish and said, "Liz, have we got any sheep dip around?"

She said, "What happened? What are you talking about?"

He said, "One of Bill Stewart's hands lost his bedroll, the mule bucked it off and it rolled down into a canyon and that was the end of that." And he said, "He crawled in with me on the last night and I've got a few fellows with me that I want to get rid of."

And she said, "What do you mean?"

He said, "I'm lousy and I need a bath and some sheep dip."

She said, "You get a wash tub and take it out on the porch."

After filling the tub full of water out of the tank on the side of stove, my mother poured in about one-half cup of sheep dip which turned the water pure white, my dad peeled off his clothes, which went into a bucket, and proceeded to give himself a scrubbing from head to toe. When he got out he said, "Well, that ought to take care of all my honored guests."

My mother said, "You could repeat the process."

My father said, "I don't think I'm going to have to. The sheep dip was strong enough that if my skin stays on I'm going to be lucky."

His skin didn't peel off, but all the fellows that he didn't need that had come home with him apparently ended up in the water; which is as it should have been.

TALES THAT STRETCH BEYOND PRESCOTT

MOUSE - IT
DEPENDS ON HOW
YOU LOOK AT IT

I learned to ride at Camp Wood. By vaquero standards, I never did really learn to ride. I did acquire a fairly steady seat and, through a great deal of tutoring by Manuel, my mother, and my father, I developed fairly good hands and a sense of balance, probably much better than the average youngster. All of this leads me to wonder what really happened when I fell off of Mouse. Mouse was a burro, sort of mouse-colored, lighter underneath than he was on his back, which led to the mouse appearance. But I really think his name originated because, according to my father, he could get through anything that a mouse could crawl through. To fence him in was almost impossible. Put him in the pasture and he always ended up in the front yard. This seemed to be one of his better characteristics.

I rode him first around the yard, and then on the lead rope, and then on my own. It was on one of these junkets that I found myself sliding gently off of Mouse and ending up on the ground. It was the first and next-to-last time that I ever fell off a horse or, that is, any horse or quadruped

that I was attempting to ride. How I fell off is only important due to what happened many years later - in 1931 to be
exact. The day that I first fell off, my mother and I were
out riding in the pasture and we stopped so she could fix
her saddle. I heard some horses behind us, slipped my
right foot out of the stirrup, turned to my left to see what
was going on, and the next thing I knew, I was headed for
the ground. Nothing really happened. Mouse stood perfectly still until I finished sliding off and then gently
stepped out of the way, that is, according to a spectator, my
mother.

In 1931, I was at Halladay's pack outfit on South Lake
in the High Sierras. Ace Reidel and I had gone there with
the intention of packing over Bishop Pass into the Kings
River country. We were talking to Halladay about starting
off the next morning and how long the pack would take. A
packer, one of Halladay's helpers, was sitting there. I did-
n't recognize him, but when I introduced myself to
Halladay, the packer asked me if I knew Bob Ferguson in
Long Beach. Since I had mentioned that that was where I
was from I said, "Yes," that Bob Ferguson was my father.

He didn't say anything more, and I didn't see him again
that afternoon. The next morning, he arrived on the scene
with a big white mule whose name, according to the name
on his pack saddle, was Blanco. He tied Blanco up to a
quaking aspen, sat down, and proceeded to roll a cigarette.

I said, "Aren't you going to pack the mule?"

He said, "If your father were here, he'd make you pack
him."

So, with that, I balanced the kyaks, put them on, and
tied the whole load on Blanco with a box hitch. When I
finished, the bearded packer looked up and said, "Not a
bad job," and with that we mounted.

He took the lead rope and off we went toward the mountain. After we had traveled about a quarter of a mile, he said, "You don't remember me, do you?"

I said, "No, I don't."

"The last time I saw you," he said, "Mouse had just bucked you off in a sand wash." The packer was Tot Young, who had worked for my father as a horse wrangler. Later he asked a lot of questions about my family. After telling him what had happened with my mother and how she had been killed in the automobile accident, I suddenly realized that he was all broken up.

The author (left) and Ace Reidel at Bishop Pass above South Lake in the Sierra Nevada Mountains at 11,964 feet. Photo taken by Tot Young. [crf]

When I told my father about meeting Tot, he also asked me many questions, "Did he have his dog and his guitar? How was he?" and "What had he been doing?" I told him as much as I could about my experience with this above-average packer.

The packer's version is the reason that the question of how I fell off of Mouse and what actually happened with Mouse is important -- at least to me, because I think I just fell off.

EPILOGUE

To get an idea of the evolution of a "tall tale," re-read the beginning of the "Reflections" section in "Reflections On Some Real and Not Very Famous Vaqueros and Cowboys." [crf]

SOME PEOPLE
WHO BUILD
RAILROADS

ARIZONA

My father spoke often of the problems and situations which confronted him in the building of railroads. After all, the building of a railroad or a canal, or for that matter a highway, is primarily a matter of moving earth. You scoop it out in the cuts and you pile it up in the fills, and when you get finished, it's leveled out to a grade. The methods, if you stop and think about it, have improved unbelievably over the years. In the 1880s the main dirt mover was a wheeled scraper.[1] This was a device built on a dropped axle with a complicated series of levers which permitted the driver to drop the scraper part of the mechanism and pick up a load of dirt, and when the scraper was full, to raise it so that the scraper moved freely on two wheels. While this resulted in a somewhat jiggling motion, it was nevertheless a rather efficient method. The only difficulty was that over a long haul the dirt that spilled out tended to raise the grade at the end of the haul, and this

---

[1] *These scrapers were called "fresnos" and were manufactured in Fresno, California. [crf]*

119

sometimes necessitated plowing it out and removing part of the grade that the scrapers themselves had developed. These new scrapers were powered by mule teams, a span of mules to a scraper. A good mule driver or mule skinner who knew how to handle a scraper was a real asset.

Most of the men who worked on the Atlantic and Pacific or Santa Fe across northern New Mexico and Arizona were either Mexicans from Old Mexico -- that is, either from Sonora or Sinaloa -- or else they were Irish. The Irish and Mexicans didn't get along very well, but they tolerated one another, and there was not a great deal of difficulty as they seldom fought one another. However, the Navajo, particularly of Northern Arizona, presented a real problem. They didn't want the A&P built along the line that now stretches from Holbrook through to the river at Needles, some of which traverses Navajo territory. The Irishmen were afraid of the Indians; the Mexicans were apprehensive, but not afraid. Their technique was to keep their scrapers together so that the mule teams were in a group, usually ten or twelve, fairly close to one another. My father always tried to find a Mexican mule driver who liked to travel at a pretty good rate. If he could put him in as a leader, then the rest of them had to keep up and the amount of dirt that was moved was considerably more than if the leader was a little more lackadaisical.

The Irishmen worked pretty much as if each one was doing the job as if he was the only mule skinner in the outfit, and he made no effort to keep an accurate distance from the one in front of him or ahead of the one behind him, but merely made sure that he didn't work too fast or too slow. The Indians, in Northern Arizona particularly, would ride up at a full gallop to where a fill or a cut was being made, stop their horses, and endeavor to kick dirt

Laying railroad track near Prescott, Arizona, ca 1890s

into the scraper drivers' faces. This was enough to almost panic the Irish. If a group of Mexicans were tightly knit, it bothered them very little. My father said the whole situation worried him for days on end. They never quite knew when they went to bed at night with their scalp whether they were going to have it the next morning or not. After all, the soldiers at Fort Apache were a long way away. It developed, of course, that the Navajos at that time were, in terms of sheep, cattle, and horses, very wealthy people. They had a lot of stock and the older and wiser Indians were very apprehensive that any sort of an attack upon the railroad builders would be devastating as far as their grazing activities were concerned, since they would probably be moved to a reservation and their freedom would be limited. It was this apprehension that restrained the younger Indians and prevented a wholesale slaughter. As it turned out, nothing really happened except a lot of people were, from time to time, very frightened.

CALIFORNIA

In California, two different groups with different ethnic backgrounds made up the Mexican community: the Mexicans from old Mexico, and the paisanos who were really native Californians, most of whom came from the area around San Juan Capistrano. These people worked for my father in the construction of the road which is now the Santa Fe between Los Angeles and San Diego. These two groups of Mexicans detested one another, and it was essential that they never be permitted in close proximity. The net result was that on any long fill, one group worked on one end and the other at the other, with plenty of room to spare in between. If they got together, even for a short time, an argument always ensued and this sometimes ended up in knife fights, the results of which were neither pretty nor pleasant for the people involved.

The Irishmen here, as in Arizona, didn't particularly care for the Mexicans, but they tolerated them, and they provided little difficulty. Most of the Irish were hired in Los Angeles. They gathered around the Old Plaza and it was there that one went looking for help. My father told me that he would drive into L.A., round up a number of prospects who claimed to be teamsters, and ship them down to wherever the railroad building was in progress. The next morning the teamster boss would round them all up and say, "Come on, boys. I'll show you your teams."

The reply of a large number was, "We didn't come down here to drive teams, we came down here to shovel."

There was no shoveling to be done; it was all work for teamsters, and they'd hired on as teamsters.

What they were really after was a cheap and easy method to get from Los Angeles to San Diego. San Diego, at that time, was in the process of development and the word had sort of gotten around that it was a beautiful place to be: a lovely city, and one which provided lots of work. This was not necessarily true, but it was, nevertheless, believed, and consequently, everyone was headed in that direction.

One of the real problems on the Los Angeles to San Diego project was the estuaries. Many of them, unlike the San Luis Rey River, were not really large enough to require bridges. Consequently, fills were used and culverts were placed to let the tide water ebb and flow. In many instances the fill was simply put across the mouth of the estuary, with the result that stingrays and other shallow water fish were trapped in the backwater. My father insists that some of the stingrays were so big that you could jab one of them with a pitchfork and that a good Irish teamster couldn't hold him down. I'm not sure this is true since I've never seen a stingray this big, but after all, who am I to doubt him? It could be that in those early days the stingrays were a little larger than they are now; if not actually larger, they may have looked larger to an Irishman with a pitchfork.

THE CHINAMAN
AND THE ABALONE

Memories are rather like views from the train window. They go slipping by, and without the ability to make notes from time to time, it's very easy to forget things that you think about. There is one incident that needs to be included in the incidents relative to the building of the Santa Fe Railroad from Los Angeles to San Diego. It is the story of the Chinaman and the abalone.

It seems that after the railroad hit the beach somewhere in the vicinity of San Juan Capistrano, after it passed through what is now the Irvine Ranch, one came upon, from time to time, a series of rocky coasts which were inhabited by many abalones. The Irishmen used to pry them loose with a shovel, dig them out of their shells, slice them real thin, and then beat them with various instruments. The cook would serve them abalone steaks deluxe.

One day the Chinaman who worked for the cook was down at the water. He passed a rock and spotted an abalone with its shell partially free of the rock. Thinking he could just snap it off, he stuck his hand under the shell and grabbed the mollusk. But the abalone wasn't having any. It clamped its shell down on the rock and the Chinaman's hand, and the Chinaman was trapped. He screamed and yelled bloody murder. The problem was that the surf was pounding on the rocks, and made a lot of noise. As a result, no one heard him. And, the tide was coming in. When this all started, the water was at his knees. It was up to his waist before someone finally spotted him, and realized what was happening. But he had to go back and find someone with a shovel. He did. The abalone was pried loose, and the Chinaman was released. The abalone became steaks.

I wasn't the one who found the Chinaman. But, I was with my father at the site when the story got back to camp. I knew the site. It was remote. The Chinaman had to have been by himself, and would have drowned if someone hadn't just happened along.

Back in those days you can bet your shirt, or at least your last five dollar gold piece, if you had been there, that if the Chinaman had been about to drown, somebody would have grabbed the Chinaman by the pigtail real hard to hold his head out of the water. To have a legitimate reason to pull a Chinaman's pigtail was an opportunity never missed, if possible.

LOS ANGELES: SNAPSHOTS OF THE LATE 1880S AND 1908

L os Angeles, in those early days, though of great importance to Southern California, was not very large as cities go. My father tells about arriving in L.A. fairly early one morning to meet his partner, McCormick, who was supposed to meet him at the railroad depot. McCormick wasn't around. My father said it didn't take him very long to find him -- there were only three restaurants in town and he knew he would be having breakfast. This gives you some idea of how the metropolis has grown since the late 1880s.

I first saw Los Angeles about 1908. In the spring when the cattle were sold, my family would usually go to Prescott; sometimes we would go to Phoenix, but on this particular occasion we came into Los Angeles. As I remember, we stayed at the Nattick House on First and Main which was one of the two or three good hotels in town; one of the others being the Van Buren, and I can't remember the third. The men's store, Mullen & Bluitt, had just opened a new store in the Storey Building at Sixth and Spring Street, and it was here that my mother took me to

Frank Ferguson in Prescott in 1910, age 6

buy a new suit. While we were shopping for the suit, my father went about his business and came back to the hotel elated. He had bought two watches, one for himself and one for my mother, which, incidentally, we still have, and a fifty dollar saddle. The saddle was made by Porter's in Phoenix, and it had been custom built for somebody who had gotten a little hard up, and sold it to a top flight saddle shop in Los Angeles. My father used the saddle for as long as he continued to ride. I understand afterwards that it rendered yeoman service on the Kinsavy Ranch for many years, and that the same tree was recovered at least three different times. This was really a quality product.

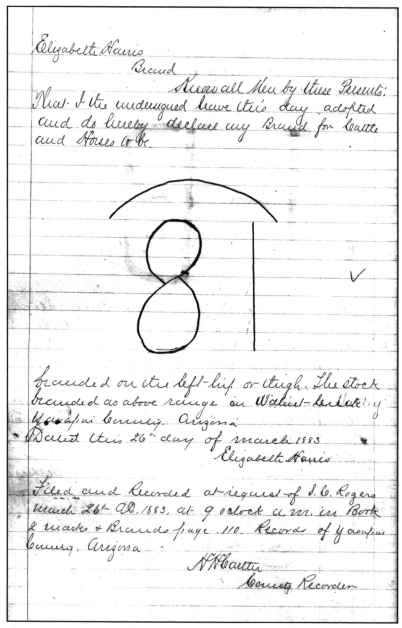

Elizabeth Harris
Brand

Know all Men by these Presents:
That I the undersigned have this day adopted
and do hereby declare my Brand for Cattle
and Horses to be.

branded on the left-hip or thigh. The stock
branded as above range in Walnut-Creek
Yavapai County, Arizona
Dated this 26th day of march 1883
Elizabeth Harris

Filed and Recorded at request of J. C. Rogers
march 26th AD, 1883, at 9 oclock a. m. in Book
2 marks & Brands page 110. Records of Yavapai
County, Arizona

N. N. Carter
County Recorder

This copy is from page 110 of Volume two of the official Yavapai County brand registry, which shows when and by whom the Quarter Circle 81 brand was registered. Note that it was registered by my grandmother Elizabeth Harris in 1883, three years before she and my grandfather were married. [crf]

BRANDS AND EARMARKS:
THE TRIAL OF T-BAR-S

Brands are read from left to right, top to bottom, and outside in. Thus, an "N" with a slanted bar diagonally across the top would be known as a Rafter N, a triangle topped by a cross would be a **N̄**　　**Ⴕ̲**　　**Ⓗ** Cross Triangle, and a circle with an "H" in the middle would be a Circle H. Reading of brands was a game played by cowboys and also by small boys. It was one of the pet pastimes in which I engaged when I was in the first and second grades in Prescott.

A great deal has been written about brands, their origin, and the legends that surround them. A brand that illustrates many of these legends, and possibly some of the mystery that surrounds some of the origins, is the XIT brand in Texas. It has been suggested that this wonderful iron was adopted because the outfit who chose it occupies ten counties in Texas. This, I believe, is factually correct. There are a number of other suggestions as to how this brand came into existence. One thought occurs that shortly after the Civil War when Texas cattlemen were in the process of branding many unbranded calves which had been born during the war and which were generally known as mavericks, the brand came into being. A young, green hand, aspiring to be a cowpuncher, asked an old cowpoke what happened and what should he do when he roped a calf. He was told to mark it. This meant branding and ear-marking it. Literally, the instructions were taken to mean: "X" was the mark which was usually used for a signature by the illiterate people. The word "it" was the "I" and "T." He "marked" "IT" and the brand came into being. This is probably incorrect, but it makes a good story. Another suggestion proposed by the author of the Time-Life Books is that the fine straight lines could be run-on by a cowboy with any small piece of metal which could be heated and held, such as a donkey shoe or a small saddle ring with a flat side held between two pieces of wood.

This brings up the two types of irons which were used in the early days. The iron primarily used on cattle which were herded together into corrals or paradas or herds was a stamp iron, the name of which is completely descriptive. The iron worked exactly like a rubber stamp, and when heated put on the entire brand. The other type of iron, used when only one or two or a small number of calves were branded, was a running iron. This has for many years been outlawed, but it was used a great deal in the early days in the cattle business. As has been said before, it could con-sist of any small piece of metal which could be heated. The XIT, which was five straight lines, lent itself beautifully to the application of a running iron.

The brand, or iron, used by the Quarter Circle 81 was a quarter circle, and underneath an 8 and a 1. Where this came from or how it originated, I have no idea.[1]

---

[1] *The brand was registered on March 26, 1883 to Dad's mother, Elizabeth Harris. This was about three years before she married my grandfather. [crf]*

Indian Joe made a type of running iron for the Quarter Circle 81 which consisted of a circle. The handle was then bent at a right angle to the circle and forged in somewhat the shape of a case knife for about six inches. The balance of the three-eighths inch Norwegian iron was permitted to extend about another six or seven inches and was then cut off and a ring was placed on the end of it. He also applied, I believe, a handle of alder wood. This iron could be used to make the 8, and then the case knife section was used for the quarter circle and the 1.

Manuel Altaininano, Ramon Contreras, and my father were trying to devise a brand which would not burn double as the 8 did where the lines crossed. Manuel drew three interlocking quarter circles in the dust. Ramon said,

"Quien sabe?" What is it? My father said, "That's what we'll register it as, Kinsavy," and this is the way you now find it in the brand books. This brand is still in existence and is owned by one of the young Neal boys who lives in Kingman.[2]

Cline, at the Yolo, saw this iron at our ranch and had Joe make a couple for him since Yolo could also be applied with exactly the same iron. The Yolo consisted of a "Y" with an "o" on one of the forks of the "Y". Two stamps makes the complete Yolo brand; so that the iron worked for him too.

The unbranded calves in Texas were known as mavericks. This name originated as the result of a San Antonio lawyer named "Maverick" taking a herd of cattle in payment of a fee. He turned them over to a black man to take care of who herded the cattle very well, but never branded any of the calves. When the outfit was sold, the buyer claimed that every unbranded calf in the country was a maverick, hence the name. It subsequently also was used to indicate a calf which was an orphan. In the western part of the United States the maverick term didn't catch on and the calves which were unbranded were known as "long ears."

The word "maverick" presents an interesting development in the American language. From a lawyer's name, in the early days, it became a term used to identify an unbranded or long-eared calf. It then became the term applied to an orphan. It now, of course, has a political significance; that is, one who is out of the mainstream of political thought or a position of a politician that is somewhat adverse to his party.

---

[2] *See registration on page 147.*

The vaquero's term for an unbranded calf is long-ear, and, as far as I know, has remained unchanged.

The stories which all of us have read relative to the altering of irons very seldom ever discuss the other problem, which was the alteration of earmarks. Every calf, when branded, was earmarked, since the earmark was also part of the indicia of ownership. The Quarter Circle 81 earmark was a swallow fork on the right and an overslope and an underbit on the left. These markings consisted of a notch cut in the right ear, the center of which was the point of the ear. It was about an inch and a half deep and it was exactly like the notch in a swallow's tail, which gave it its name, Swallow fork. The overslope was merely the cutting of a portion of the upper part of the left ear so that, rather than being curved, it was flat on the top. The underbit was made by inserting a knife about two-thirds of the way between the point of the ear and the calf's head, making a cut about a quarter of an inch deep back to the edge of the ear and then cutting a straight line at right angles to this cut to the other edge of the ear. This left a flare area at the bottom of the ear which was known as the bit.

When a calf was branded it was earmarked, and if the brand was to be altered the earmark also had to be altered or the original earmark was a dead giveaway as to the alteration of the brand. One of the processes that went on in the early days when hands were few and far between, was one known as sleepering. The average cowpuncher, be he cowboy or vaquero, riding up to a cow and a calf, examined the calf's ears. Rather than looking for a brand, if the calf was earmarked the chances were he was branded. This led to a rustling process known as sleepering which consisted of earmarking a calf but not branding him. The earmark that was carried by the cow was placed on the calf, the cuts being made as small as possible so that it could later be altered. When the calf was big enough to be weaned, he was re-earmarked and branded with the iron of the knave who had improperly earmarked him in the first place. The term "sleepering," I believe, comes from the faro game where a sleeper was a bet on a dead card.

Subsequently, when the ranchers were able to operate with adequate help, this process was practically ended, since the calves could be more carefully examined. And, actually a higher percentage were rounded up and branded in the initial round-up or rodeos.

All this miscellaneous information is of little use, but nevertheless interesting. There was one time, however, when a young lawyer[3] found himself engaged in a trial that was considerably different than what was anticipated. It seems that the daughter of a prominent Los Angeles family married a young man who had grown up in the San Joaquin Valley on one of the big cattle ranches. They had a ranch in the Tehachapi Mountains with a winter range that spread down into the Mojave Desert. It adjoined a ranch used by a grouchy old character who was disliked by most of the other ranchers, farmers, and people generally, in Tehachapi. It seems that it was the old character's practice to claim everything in sight. On this particular occasion he accused the young woman and her husband of branding three of his calves, and proceeded to bring an action to get them back.

The couple was represented by a young lawyer who was a member of one of the big law firms in Los Angeles which represented the corporation owned by the young woman's family.

The plaintiff's lawyer called the codger to the stand and

---

[3] *My Dad modestly described himself in the third person. [crf]*

asked him about the calves and identified a picture of three calves. Plaintiff claimed that they were his and that they had been branded by the defendants and that they were his property. The pictures did not clearly indicate the brands, but he testified that they were the brand which was "run" by the young woman and her husband; in this case the T-Bar-S. With that, the plaintiff rested.

The defendants' lawyer took on the plaintiff for cross-examination. The first question he asked him was if he had pictures of the cows which were the supposed mothers of the three calves. Of course he didn't. Plaintiff was then asked whether the brands were put on with a running iron or a stamp iron. To this question plaintiff surprisingly had no answer. He then was asked if he had carefully examined the earmarks to see whether or not they had been altered or whether or not they were the original earmarks. He testified that he believed that they were the original earmarks, and every one of the calves had not been sleepered. On this, the brand inspector's ears perked up, and he started to pay rather careful attention to what was going on.

The attorney for the defense then dismissed plaintiff and called the defendants. They denied that the calves were the calves of the plaintiff, and said they had been born of T-Bar-S cows and branded with T-Bar-S stamp irons. The calves in question at the time were practically yearlings. The defense then called the Inspector of Brands and asked him if he had inspected the brands. He said that he had. On further questioning, he stated that they had been put on with a stamp iron. He was then asked if there was a foolproof way to tell if a brand had been altered. He said there was. You had to kill the animal, skin it, and look at the flesh side. This would indicate clearly if the brand had been altered. This, of course, had not and could not, in this case, be done. The defendants' attorney then rested. He then argued to the Judge that the plaintiff had not met his burden of proof. Plaintiff had not shown that there had been any alteration of the brand. The earmarks were original and had not been sleepered. Plaintiff had not shown that the brands had been applied to cattle that were his.

The Judge took the matter under advisement and two days later handed down a decision for the defendants. In other words, the cattle stealing case, which the plaintiff had hoped that he could lodge against the T-Bar-S owners, went out the window. The ranchers in Tehachapi cheered to themselves and to one another that the old codger had received his just desserts and would no longer be bothering the ranchers around Tehachapi. The owners of the T-Bar-S went happily about their business.

The codger was especially unhappy. Not only had he been bested, but he had been bested by someone he thought was a city boy.

THOUGHTS ON RANGE WARS - MOVIES AND NOVELS

FOREWORD

My Dad was born well after the Pleasant Valley War in Pleasant Valley and the Tonto Basin War, in Yavapai County. But those and the Lincoln County War in New Mexico were the constant source of material for books and movies. And because Dad was in the movie business for thirty-one years, he had to include something about a subject that he had been exposed to, that kept coming up at the Studio. [crf]

RANGE WARS, NOVELS AND MOVIES

When Tot Young[2] left my father's ranch to work for the Cross Triangle, he guided the western novelist Harold Bell Wright around, and actual-

---

[2] *Described in "Reflections On Some Real and Not Very Famous Vaqueros and Cowboys" and "Mouse". [crf]*

ly helped him locate the string of wild horses that ranged on Granite Mountain, which dominates the Williamson's Valley area. Those who have read *When a Man's a Man,* which was a novel that Wright wrote with the Valley as its locale, will remember the Cross Triangle Ranch and the owner. The owner was actually Bill Stuart who was one of my father's good friends and who was reported to have arrived in Arizona in the early days with his Levis patched with a flour sack that said across the back, "Pillsbury's Best."

Wright had intended to write a novel concerning the Pleasant Valley War (which was sometimes referred to as the Tonto Basin War), which had been a vicious feud that had gone on for many years between two families, the Tewksburys and the Grahams. It also involved the ongoing battle between the sheep men and the cattlemen, who were trying to drive the sheep men out of Tonto Basin and out of a large part of Arizona.

This feud involved many people in high places in Arizona and was little discussed, though it was bitter and vicious. Rod Burnham's father, in his book *Scouting on Two Continents*, refers to it and discusses some of the things that he took part in, although all of his material is quite veiled and he doesn't actually reveal anyone who was involved. Rod and I have compared notes from time to time, and we found that neither of us really knew anything about the Pleasant Valley War except that it existed and that it eventually ended. According to Zane Gray, the last man married the last girl and everything was happy after that. According to my father, the last man killed was shot in Phoenix while riding on a grain wagon. I'm not sure whether he was a cattleman or a sheep man.

Another war which is famous throughout the West is

the Lincoln County War. It was these two conflicts that formed the basis for much of the fiction that has been written about the feuds between families and the cattlemen and sheep men. The Lincoln County War served as a basis for the John Wayne picture entitled *Chisholm*. In that picture William Bonnie, Billy the Kid, rode off into the sunset; but, as we all know, he was actually killed by Pat Garrett.

THE MAIN HOUSE BURNS - THE BEGINNING OF THE END

It was the winter that the log house, which had been the landmark at Camp Wood for many years, caught fire and burned. Exactly how it happened I'm not sure. But as I remember it, everyone was gone from the ranch except my mother and father, and he was out in the barn shucking corn since the fodder had all been carted into the barn and the loft was full of hay. My mother sensed something was wrong and ran outside and discovered that the house was on fire where one of the stovepipes went through the wall to the outside. Apparently the insulation had broken down and the heat from the winter fire (there were about two inches of snow on the ground) had been sufficient to ignite the siding. She tried to call my father, who was some distance away. When he finally realized that something was wrong, he came running. He always swore that we threw the dishes out the window and carried out the bedding. But nevertheless quite a few things were removed from the house. Some of my toys were saved. I remember a great deal of my mother's dishes, a large quantity of bedding and some of the furniture. This was left out in the snow and we spent the rest of the night in the bunkhouse, which was vacant and available.

In watching the fire burn I can remember the shelves which contained not only store-bought canned goods but vegetables which had been canned, that is, put up in Mason jars for use in the winter. As the heat consumed the building, these jars fell from the shelves and either exploded or crashed to the floor. My mother was practically in tears -- the house and all the jellies, the jams, the preserves that had been so laboriously put up in the fall were gone. Datewise, I believe this catastrophe occurred in the winter of 1910.

The blacksmith's shop was much larger than was needed, and my father quickly decided that a large portion of it could be used as a makeshift dwelling. An examination of the ruins of the house revealed that the wood stove, that is, the cooking stove, was still usable and could be moved and made available. The fireplace was built in the north end of the blacksmith shop. A partition was put in so that the part that had formerly been the shop itself, which contained the anvils, the forge, and all that type of equipment, was partitioned off from the balance. This made a room similar to a large living room. The bunkhouse was altered and a portion of the building that had been used as a storage space for meat and other supplies was incorporated into the bunkhouse. What had formerly been the bunkhouse and a portion of the blacksmith shop became the living quarters for my family.

Cheng moved into the new bunkhouse area and, outside of a slight inconvenience to everyone, life went on about as usual.

Everyone pitched in and excavated a rectangular area in a hillside which was only about ten or fifteen yards from the blacksmith shop. The cellar was constructed here, with a cement wall which lined the inside of the hillside. Then the structure was roofed over with rafters (poles) and I think probably a sod roof, although I'm not certain. It provided storage space for practically everything that had to be stored in a cool, dry place. It was really an improvement in some respects over what had been used before. The only problem was that there was some seepage and it didn't drain out quite as well as desired. This was corrected. They drilled a few down-slanting holes in the wall at proper places at floor level, and from then on the cellar performed in admirable fashion.

LEAVING CAMP WOOD

On November 7, 1910, I started school at the Lincoln School on the west side of Prescott. November 7 is my birthday, and I was six years old. I didn't have any trouble keeping up with the class since my mother had given me a pretty thorough training, using one of the early McGuffy readers. I had learned most of the rudimentary arithmetic combinations and my writing was better than passable. Spelling was a problem even in first grade and it followed me all the rest of my life--I still can't spell my own name without thinking about it.

In June of 1912, I finished the second grade and with grades that were nearly all fours, which were equivalent to A's in those days. I took my report card and hurried up the hill, past the Murphy house, to show it to my mother since I had been promised a possible trip to the railroad if I had good grades. A trip to the railroad meant that I would be able to go on the cattle drive from Camp Wood. I walked in the door and suddenly realized that the man with my mother in the living room who was dressed in a dark grey suit, a grey flannel shirt, a black necktie, and shoes instead of boots was my father, who was not quite as tall as I'd always thought he was. I'd never seen him in anything in the way of foot gear except his Blucher boots.

He scooped me up and said, "I'm glad to see you. What have you here?" I showed him my report card and he said, "Wonderful, you'll need it where we're going."

I said, "Where are we going?"

He said, "To California. We've sold the ranch."

I'm certain my face fell a foot. He went on to explain that the Quarter Circle 81 cattle were to be moved to Boar Creek, combined with the FD's and that in the future the Kinsavy iron, with which we were all familiar, would be used.

The cattle company which he and John Neal and two other men had organized would operate the Kinsavy Cattle Company.[1] John would be the foreman. It seems that Manuel and Ramon would stay with the cattle, and Cheng had agreed to stay with the cattle company if its owners

Ramon Contreras ultimately worked at the Yolo Ranch. He is seen here (at the far left) in the roundup crew of the Yolo Ranch ca 1945.

Photo from the collection of Mona Lange McCroskey

---

[1] See: *"Brand Book and Livestock Laws of the State of Arizona - Ordered, Compiled and Printed by The Arizona Live Stock Sanitary Board, March 25th, 1916, page 337.*

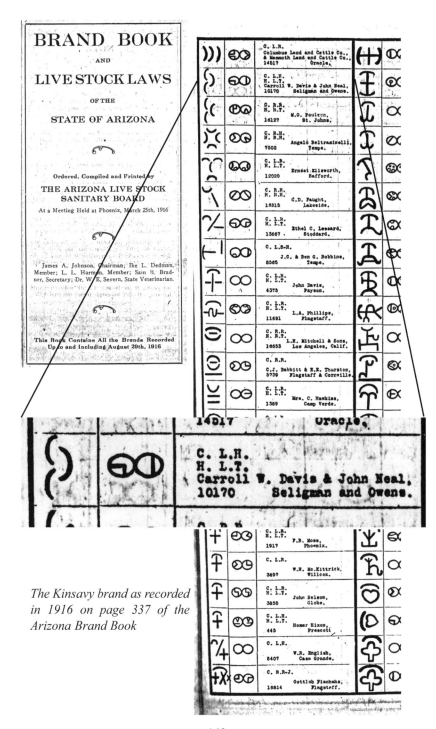

The Kinsavy brand as recorded in 1916 on page 337 of the Arizona Brand Book

149

would send his body back to China when he died. This was agreed to. Ed had evidenced some indication that he wanted to go back to see his people, although he had been offered a job by the Cross Triangle and also the Yolo. He was an excellent hand and as such was much in demand.

Joe, during the last year, had been real busy braiding riatas and headstalls for bridles, also making bridle conchas and inlaying spurs for customers that came to him requesting products. At my father's suggestion and with some encouragement from one of the bankers in Prescott, Joe planned to set up his own business. The banker was to help him with the bookkeeping and all the clerical details, and Joe would also have the help of a couple of young, ambitious Hualapais. This was an excellent situation for him, and it also gave the two young Indians an opportunity to act as apprentices at a business that was rapidly passing from the scene, but which, nevertheless, enjoyed a great demand among the discerning cowpunchers in the whole area. Joe's products were very much in demand and during the last year he had practically refused to take any wages from the Quarter Circle 81 since most of his time had been devoted to working for people who came to him seeking the products that he manufactured and did so beautifully.[2] I understand that he was highly successful.

This, for me, was the end of an era and a way of life.

---

[2] *The lightweight riata that Joe made for my Dad still hangs on our wall. It was probably tied to Dad's saddle when he fell (or was thrown) off of Mouse. [crf]*

THE FINAL
CHAPTER

Every year after we left Arizona my father returned in the spring or early summer at roundup time and spent anywhere from a week to two weeks at the cattle company. I accompanied him in 1918. We took the train from Los Angeles to Kingman, and from Kingman we drove to the Big Sandy where we spent a few days with my mother's sister and her family. We then rode horseback overland from Big Sandy to Burro Creek. We packed our gear on pack animals and it was a long, hard day's ride. We arrived in Burro Creek to find that the roundup crew was working in an area known as Goodwin Mesa, which was a rimrock country not too far away and which provided beautiful pasture for the stock. A large area could be enclosed with only a few fences, since most of the area was inaccessible except in one or two places. A large corral had been built on the top of the mesa, and it was here that the roundup was taking place.

Manuel and Ramon were there, and some other cowpunchers who worked for the Kinsavy outfit. We spent a couple of days in the cow camp and then came back to

Burro Creek, where we enjoyed approximately a week's riding and rodeoing with the crew. I got a big kick out of it because it was my first real roundup since we had left Camp Wood.

We drove into Congress Junction, visited a few days with the Darnells, and then took the train to Prescott. When we arrived in Prescott and emerged from the depot my father said, "This town is really jumping. I hope Shorty Davis took care of our accommodations." I wondered about the baggage and he said, "We'll send for it," and proceeded to walk up Cortez toward Gurley.

At the corner of Gurley and Cortez he said, "Look who's here."

I didn't recognize the man that he met but it turned out that it was Pete White of the "big-footed bear incident." White had sold a mine to the United Verde, taken back some stock as part of the purchase agreement, and when United Verde was acquired by Anaconda, had come into quite a bit of money. He was living at the Pioneers' Home and really enjoying life. We proceeded up Gurley Street to the Yavapai Club and went in. The men behind the desk looked up and said, "I didn't expect two of you. I hope you can sleep in a double bed."

My dad laughed and said, "That'll present no problem." He gave the bellboy three dollars, the baggage checks, and told him to collect the two suitcases and a rifle case which was at the depot. The rifle case was a .22 repeating Remington which was my pride and joy and which I had used to shoot jackrabbits at Burro Creek.

The next morning we had breakfast at the Chinaman's and then went into Garrett's Barber Shop. My father got a shave, I got a haircut, and we proceeded to the fairgrounds since the Frontier Days celebration had just begun. There were many more people there than I remembered, fancier saddles and groups of performers which were not present at the earlier functions I had attended as a small boy. When the Frontier Days ended we said goodbye to our friends in Prescott, which included the group from the Kinsavy ranch.

When my father said goodbye to Manuel, I realized how deep was their respect and affection for each other. A long handshake -- two handed, almost ritualistic -- then the goodbye, softly, it seemed, in unison, "Goodbye, Manuel," "Vaya con Dios, Uncle Bob." Their eyes met for an instant, then each turned and walked away. I can still remember the blink to fight back the tears. I don't believe they ever met again, the young, talented vaquero and the worldly old cattleman. Later we caught the train back to Los Angeles. As we settled into our seats my father said, "I wonder. This is almost too good to last. We've had no droughts, no bad years for flies, and the price of cattle has done nothing but go up. All I can say is I hope it continues."

It didn't. Now, looking back, I think he sensed what was to come. The four years of droughts, dry water holes, and other catastrophes are history.

My father never went back to Arizona again.

GLOSSARY

Adz - A tool with an arched blade at right angle to the handle. Used for shaping wood.

Anvil - A block of iron or steel with a flat top upon which metal is shaped by hammering. One end that comes to a point for shaping horseshoes.

Auger - A tool for boring holes in wood with a sharp end for cutting and spiral grooves for channeling the shavings out.

Beeves - (*pl.*) An alternate term for beef. Sometimes used instead of "cattle."

Bit - The metal mouthpiece attached to the bridle. Contains a bar that is inserted in the horse's mouth, and the rings to which the reins are attached.

Brand - The mark of ownership. Made with a hot iron on the hides of beeves.

Bridle - A horse's headgear consisting of the crown piece across the top of the head behind the ears, the brow band across the forehead, cheek pieces on each side of the horse's head, and the throat-latch. The bit and reins are attached.

Branding Iron - A metal rod with a specifically-designed end used for burning brands on the hides of beeves.

Buckaroo - Cowboy. A perversion of the term vaquero.

Bunk house - The place where ranch hands live, not unlike barracks.

155

Bushwhacker - Generally, one who shoots another from an ambush. A thief or robber who masquerades as someone who would otherwise be respected, such as a Civil War veteran.

Case knife - a hunting knife kept in a case or sheath.

Center-fire rig - A saddle with one cinch.

Chaps - Leather leggings worn over a cowboy's trousers or Levis to protect him from thorns or rain.

Chinking - Closes up narrow cracks or fissures.

Cinch - A broad band of woven horsehair, canvas or ropes, usually about 4 inches wide, which extends under the horse's belly to secure the saddle.

Cinch ring - A large ring at each end of the cinch, which with the latigo, is used to secure the cinch to the saddle.

Conchas (also spelled conchos) - A silver or metal ornament, often attached to a bridle.

Corral - A large pen, usually round and without corners constructed of wood rails and posts.

Cowboy or Cowpuncher - An employee of a cattleman or rancher whose primary work is performed riding a horse.

Cutting horse - A horse that by instinct and training is able to separate a specific head of cattle from the herd.

Dally (also dallying) - To take a wrap around the saddle horn. Normally it is done with a rope after roping a calf to make it secure. At the Frontier Day race in Prescott, it was done with the latigo to make the saddle secure.

Dutch oven - (*1*) As used on the Quarter Circle 81 a square metal container for roasting meats, etc., with its open side facing the fire. (*2*) Generally, a heavy cast iron pot with three legs/feet and a heavy, tight lid. It could not only be placed on the fire, but hot coals could be placed on its lid.

Earmark - A cut or notch made in the ear(s) of beeves to show ownership.

Faro - (from Pharaoh, an old French card design.) Popular in the west in the 19th century. To play, all of the spades are laid out face up on the table. Bets are then placed on these cards. The cards are then turned by the dealer from the top (hopefully) of the deck. Two cards are drawn. The first is a win for the dealer, the second a win for the player. For example, if the player places a bet on the five, and the dealer turns a five on the first card, he wins. If a five comes up on the second card, player wins. If the cards turned by the dealer are a 4 and 10, nothing happens on the 5 bets, yet.

Forge - A furnace where a blacksmith heats metal.

Hackamore - A halter that has reins instead of a lead rope, and becomes a bridle without a bit. The horse is controlled by pressure on its neck.

Hand - A unit of measurement for measuring the height of horses. It was originally the width of a man's palm. Now it is normally 4 inches.

Headstall - A bridle.

High port bit - One of the more severe bits that places pressure on the soft portion of a horse's tongue or pallet when the horse is reined.

Horse wrangler - During roundup, the person (often a boy) responsible for keeping the saddle horses from going too far astray or rounding them up, usually in the morning. Also, a cowboy (commonly known as a "bronc buster") who broke horses for riding.

Jerky - Dried beef made by slicing it into strips before drying it in the sun.

Kyacks - Large canvas container bags (packsacks) that are hung on either side of a pack saddle.

Lasso - (*v.*) To catch an animal with a long rope with a running noose. (*n.*) The rope or riata used to catch the animal.

Latigo - A long leather strap which attached the rigging of a saddle to the cinch. It hangs from a ring called a rigging tree or saddle ring, which is passed through the cinch ring and back up successively until tight and then tied with a knot that resembles a four-in-hand on a necktie.

Low port bit - A bit that is relatively gentle and places only a little pressure on the horse's tongue when it is reined.

Maverick - An unbranded calf.

Muley - Hornless or poled cattle.

Neck rein - To guide a horse with one hand by using the rein to put pressure on the horse's neck. By moving the hand and the reins to the left, pressure is put on the right side of the horse's neck toward the left and the horse turns to the left.

Needle-Gun - A breach loading, as opposed to muzzle loading, rifle invented in Prussia in the mid 1800s. The loading mechanism was similar to today's bolt action rifle.

Orejana - Unbranded cattle.

Paisano - A person of Mexican descent who was born outside of Mexico; for example, in Arizona or California.

Parada - Cattle in a group or herd. Taken from the term parada grounds which means the area selected for holding a herd after a roundup.

Rawhide - Dried skin or hide. Prepared by soaking it in water, and usually removing the hair. It is not treated with chemicals.

Rein - (*n.*) A narrow strap of leather attached to each end of the bit, and held by the rider to control the horse. (*v.*) A means of guiding, controlling checking or restraining the horse.

Riata (also spelled Reata) - A rope made from braided rawhide.

Rimmy (also rimmies) - A saddle with two cinches.

Rowel - The revolving disc at the end of a spur that touches the horse. The points vary from long and pointed in the Mexican tradition to the small, dull and flower-like pattern that was developed in Texas.

Roundup - Gathering cattle. Used for such things as gathering stray beeves, or gathering them for branding or for shipment to market.

Running iron - An individually designed branding iron. The one at the Quarter Circle 81 consisted of a rod that is curved at one end. The one at the Yolo Ranch consisted of a circle. They were used by a ranch to create its brand, or by a rustler to change a brand.

Sharps rifle - A breach loading, single shot rifle manufactured by Christian Sharps at calibers from .36 to .52, and said to be accurate at long distances. 45/70 refers to the caliber, and the size of the cartridge.

Sheep dip - Any chemical preparation used as a bath to free sheep from vermin and sheep scab, or to clean the fleece and skin before sheering.

Shock - To stack sheaves of corn or wheat upright for drying.

Slash - The clutter of branches, chips or other debris from the cutting of timber or removal of bark.

Sleepering - The practice of placing shallow earmarks and no brand on a calf so that the person could later come back and change the earmarks and brand the calf with his own iron.

Snaffle bit - Also called a grazing bit, it generally consists of two short bars joined in the middle of the horse's mouth that brings a minimum amount of pressure on the horse's tongue. It is considered very gentle.

Snake - To drag or pull a log with a rope attached at one end.

Stirrups - Foot supports for the saddle. Generally made from wood with metal reinforcement.

Stamp iron - A branding iron with the owner's entire brand or pattern at the "business end."

Tapaderos - Leather covers over the front and sides of the stirrups that protected the rider's boots.

Tree - The basic hardwood frame for a saddle.

Vaquero - A person of Mexican descent who was either a cavalryman or trained in that manner of riding and herding, and whose skills were well above those of an average Mexican cowboy.